To Richard,   July 1988

   What a wonderful, delightful time we've had — playing house!

         With much affection,
         Bob Perkins

GRAND ILLUSIONS

CONTEMPORARY INTERIOR MURALS

Caroline Cass

With photographs by Tom Leighton

PHAIDON · OXFORD

for Alain

Phaidon Press Limited, Littlegate House,
St Ebbe's Street, Oxford, OX1 1SQ
First published 1988
© Phaidon Press Limited, 1988

British Library Cataloguing in Publication
Data
Cass, Caroline
  Grand illusions: contemporary interior
  murals.
  1. Mural painting and decoration
  I. Title
  751.7′3   ND2550

  ISBN 0–7148–2481–X

Printed in Spain by Heraclio
Fournier SA, Vitoria

Endpapers. Graham Rust.
Sketch drawing. 1976.
Inkwash, 21 × 14·7 cm (8¼ × 5¾ in).
Artist's collection

Half-title. Christian Thee. *Lilies in
Bloom*. 1976. Acrylic on wood,
285 × 190 cm (108 × 72 in). Private
collection

Frontispiece. Robert Walker. 1971.
Acrylic, 2·85 × 14·26 m (9 × 45 ft)
(*detail*). Richard Booth. See also
Plates 93 and 94

1. Roy Alderson. 1959. Acrylic and oil
   on board and brick, 792 × 475 cm
   (300 × 180 in). Artist's collection

2. (*overleaf*) Graham Rust. *The
   Temptation*. 1969–83. Indelible
   gouache on rag paper. Marquess of
   Hertford, Ragley Hall, Warwickshire

CONTENTS

3. Andrea Mantegna. *Camera degli Sposi*, Palazzo Ducale, Mantua. 1465–74

4. Garth Benton. 1986. Acrylic, 4·75 × 12·67 m (15 × 40 ft). Mrs Ann Getty

INTRODUCTION

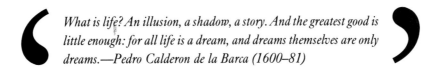

What is life? An illusion, a shadow, a story. And the greatest good is little enough: for all life is a dream, and dreams themselves are only dreams.—Pedro Calderon de la Barca (1600–81)

This book is about English and American murals and the artists who paint them. There is a wealth of talented muralists in both countries, working in a rich variety of styles, who are producing exuberant works of art. Murals are one branch of the visual arts which cannot easily be exhibited in their original form and this book provides an insight into the largely unknown, often unheralded and sometimes magnificent world of wallpaintings. After languishing for decades in the backwaters of the art world, the mural is making a remarkable comeback.

The painted mural is both an ancient and a modern art. From its roots in prehistory, through the splendour of the Renaissance and Baroque periods, to the challenging and vital 1930s, the art form has been nurtured and admired. Art began with wallpainting, and although muralists may no longer dip their sticks in wood ash and natural clay pigment as they did fifteen thousand years ago, the urge to transform our surroundings has never left us.

Murals are a skilful attempt at illusion. They expand our horizons and provide an extra dimension to our instinctive need to dream and fantasize. The common wall provides an opportunity for this to be achieved on a heroic scale. On a more basic level, the mural is a decorative work for a specific area to expand the space we live in. At its finest it should be a continuation of architecture. At its most inspired, it is art, representing the essence of a great cultural tradition such as the work of the Italian masters, Michelangelo, Veronese and Tiepolo, in the sumptuous palaces and churches of Italy. A mural should have intrinsic as well as decorative merit, though this is not always achieved.

The last two decades of passionate involvement in embellishing our surroundings with colour and texture, patterns and paint is the result of a palpable reaction against the sterile walls and bare spaces of postwar architecture.

INTRODUCTION

This renaissance of the mural has come about as artists, architects and an increasingly art-conscious public realize that collaboration on beautifying buildings can only enhance our surroundings.

Contemporary muralists are multi-faceted and skilled painters, eager to tackle any style of architecture and any rooms whose awkward dimensions present a problem. Many of the great artists of the past—Titian, Picasso, Matisse—painted murals, and most of the muralists featured in this book also work in other mediums. The best are always in demand. Relatively few make their living solely from murals and often they enjoy the diversity and challenge of jumping from large-scale commissions to working in a smaller dimension. The urge to make our houses and buildings more attractive, a nostalgia for the past, the challenge of working on a huge scale and the large amount of money offered to the best muralists, especially in America, have all contributed to the mural's current popularity.

The private mural has been influenced and encouraged by the proliferation of public works in the past two decades on both sides of the Atlantic: political murals inspired by the radical spirit of the late 1960s in pop art and graffiti, religious murals, publicly funded and spontaneous community art wallpaintings done to brighten up drab urban environments. It was a natural step to look inwards and to create a finer alternative in the decoration of our homes and places of work.

The American muralists included in the book work mainly on the East and West coasts—New York, Los Angeles and San Francisco. Many of the sensibilities of England and New York come from a shared tradition of looking towards Europe for inspiration. Los Angeles is entirely different. Its progressive architecture, huge spaces and bright light, plus the influence of its Spanish past, lend themselves better to exterior murals, large, vibrant works commissioned for public spaces.

Wallpainting tends to be at its best when associated with great architecture and, once again, the balance between art and architecture seems to be restoring itself. Modern buildings, especially in Britain, are often unattractive and characterless and rarely have an identifiable style. Murals create this and lend character where none exists. Architects who are no longer anxious about losing control of their work are beginning to include muralists in the planning stages of a building.

Muralists have, traditionally, been inspired by a limited number of classical themes, such as religion, the four seasons, historical events, the hunt and the ages of man. The predominant driving force for wallpainting, though, has been religion, as witnessed in early Christian, Byzantine and medieval wallpaintings. In the fifteenth century art was also almost entirely devoted to the glorification of God and the Church and it was a visual language in which the masters expressed themselves fluently.

Besides having a wider range of subjects to choose from, the modern muralist has another advantage over his ancestor—the wealth of materials available. In addition to paint, mosaics and stained glass, which have always been used, muralists now employ ceramics, enamel, weavings, wood and stone carvings, metals and plastics to enhance their work. Occasionally several mediums are combined in a single work.

The origins of contemporary murals lie deep in prehistory, when cavemen etched ritual images of their lives with the crudest of implements. The fascination with the decoration of buildings continued with Egyptian art and the frescoes painted in the city of Pompeii. These delicate wallpaintings were preserved in volcanic ash following the eruption of Mount Vesuvius in 79 AD. Most important buildings at that time had painted walls, and the Greek and Roman elite were the first to have rooms in their fine villas decorated and enlarged by depicting loggias, columns and painted windows looking out onto distant vistas. The most sumptuous of all villas was the Golden House, built for Nero in Rome between 64 and 68 AD. The opulent interior was filled with intricate mosaics, frescoes painted by Fabullus, costly marbles and Nero's famous art collections. The Golden House also possessed exquisite stuccoes modelled in relief. Some examples from that period have managed to survive in tombs and grottoes—from which

5. Giambattista Tiepolo. *The Banquet of Antony and Cleopatra.* 1747–50. (Painted architectural decoration by G. Mengozzi-Colonna).
Palazzo Labia, Venice

comes the word 'grotesque' for describing this type of decorative motif.

Scientific perspective was first mastered during the Italian Renaissance, by the Florentine architects, Filippo Brunelleschi (1377–1446) and Leon Battista Alberti (1404–72). This discovery revolutionized the study of art and architecture, allowing the artist to break through the wall and create an imaginary space beyond, thus producing the birth of the true three-dimensional mural. The first important artist who applied Brunelleschi's innovation in his paintings was Masaccio (1401–28). Three years before his early death at the age of twenty-seven, Masaccio elaborately used perspective in his painting *The Holy Trinity, with the Virgin, St John and Donors*. Thereafter, perspective became a basic principle of every succeeding generation of artists. One of the highlights of Renaissance illusionistic decoration was the superb fresco painted by Andrea Mantegna (c.1431–1506) in the Camera degli Sposi, in the ducal palace of Mantua, between 1465 and 1474 (Plate 3). Mantegna pierced the centre of the dome by painting an open oculus as an infinite blue sky with playful cherubs and figures in period costume peering down over a balustrade. He was the first of the great painters intent on achieving an image of limitless space.

True fresco (*fresco buono*) was the painting technique which was most extensively used during the Renaissance. Pigments ground with water are painted onto a wet lime plaster surface and the colour is incorporated into the chemical structure of the plaster as it cures, thus becoming a part of the wall. In this sense fresco was used as an architectural medium. Today true frescoes are seldom done, and acrylic and oil paints have taken their place.

The involvement of architecture and art was at its closest during the highly ornate and sensuous Baroque and Rococo periods with their sense of theatre. By the Baroque period, there were few aspects of the difficulties in mural painting which had not been conquered. This was not so with the Romans, who, not having mastered perspective, designed their frescoes as purely illusionist, although effective decorations. The greatest achievements of the Baroque era were the many splendid ceiling paintings, and Giambattista Tiepolo, a master at them, was the finest decorative painter of eighteenth-century Europe. He continues to be a major inspiration to many of the artists in this book. One of his best-known frescoes (c.1747) was painted in the Palazzo Labia at Venice, in which he depicted two scenes from the love story of Antony and Cleopatra. One of the paintings shows a sumptuous banquet at which Cleopatra bet her lover she would preside over the most expensive feast ever given. She won her wager by dropping one of her priceless pearl earrings into vinegar, where it dissolved (Plate 5).

Britain and America in the eighteenth century were never at ease with the excesses of the Rococo, favouring instead the more severe style of Palladianism, named after the architectural principles of Andrea Palladio (1508–80). The inheritance of Palladio's buildings, which were modelled on the temples of the ancients and which had a commanding influence over interior design in Britain, gave way to the Neo-classical style in the mid-eighteenth century. Inspired by the excavations at Pompeii and Herculaneum after 1750, its aim was to copy or emulate the different styles of art established in the ancient world.

Following in the tradition of the Rococo period, Italian Neo-classical decoration inclined towards large frescoes over the walls and ceilings of palaces and villas. Among the most popular Neo-classical frescoists was Felice Giani (1758–1823) whose work in the gallery of the Palazzo Zacchia-Laderchi at Faenza was one of the highlights of the period. This use of frescoes and large decorative paintings continued into Italy's Romantic period. The English architect and interior designer Robert Adam (1728–92) epitomized English Neo-classicism in his 'Etruscan' decoration at Osterley Park House (c.1775–79). Having studied the art, architecture and decoration of the Italians, and mastered the 'grotesque' ornamentations, Adam longed to replace the heaviness of British Palladianism with a light and graceful touch. Osterley Park contains the best examples of his style of decoration derived from the grotesque, set against his favourite pale pastel colours and interspersed with exquisite inset paintings.

A taste for the picturesque led away from the severity of Neo-classicism to the quixotic Romantic period.

6. Mary Adshead. Beaverbrook mural: *Newmarket Ring*. 1928. Oil on canvas, 208 × 328 cm (78 × 124 in). Mr and Mrs David Abbot

The essence of the age of Romanticism in nineteenth-century Europe and Britain was its interpretive freedom which relied on past styles, such as Gothic, Byzantine, Moorish, Chinoiserie and Renaissance in order to awaken certain emotional responses in the viewer.

Whereas the Europeans have had centuries on which to build, the American tradition of wallpainting evolved in the late eighteenth and early nineteenth centuries, probably as a reaction to the religious prejudice against all forms of art and luxurious living. Painted by self-taught craftsmen and itinerant artists, many of whom were immigrants from the more cultured world of Europe, these simple and harmonious wallpaintings possessed an appealing freshness. They were essentially a folk art with a sensitivity which had little to do with the technique of great mural painting but instead concentrated on lightness of colour and simplicity of design for effect. Examples of this type of wallpainting still survive in New England, but many of the artists were anonymous, and even the names of specific artists such as the itinerant painter, William Price, are not widely known.

Whether a major work of art or purely decorative, in beautiful houses or functional offices, the mural is a fascinating and pleasing art form, drawing us out of our everyday lives into a world of illusion and delight.

7. Mary Adshead. Beaverbrook mural: *Picnic on the way to Newmarket*. 1928. Oil on canvas, 208 × 197 cm (78 × 75 in). Mr and Mrs David Abbot

8. Thomas Hart Benton. *America Today*. 1930. 30 m (95 ft). The Equitable Life Assurance Society of the United States, New York

MURALS IN THE 1930s

Murals in the turbulent 1930s tended to be politically and socially inspired. At a time of financial and political insecurity, marked by a world depression and culminating in World War II, the fusion between reality and illusion became visually more pronounced. People needed to escape. These were stirring times, and art was influenced, and also destroyed, by monumental political events. Nazi Germany, Mussolini's Italy and Stalin's Russia systematically crushed the artistic avant-garde of each country. In the United States, on the other hand, large-scale government patronage of the visual arts following the Depression encouraged an entire generation of creative talent.

The impetus for the boom in American mural art was inspired mainly by what was happening south of the border, in Mexico. Here was a revolutionary art, addressing itself directly to the people of Mexico, which had exploded upon the country in the previous decade. This dynamic school of mural painting was known as Mexican Muralism. It was based on a rising tide of nationalism and had begun soon after the revolution which spawned the most powerful national school of mural painting since the Italian Renaissance and the first important modern art movement created outside Europe.

Mural painting also took hold as a populist art in Italy and the United States, and to a lesser extent in England. Social upheaval, interminable dole queues, the extremes of wealth and poverty during the Depression, and the lasting effects of the Great War all contributed to a crisis of identity and had an immense impact on the relationship between the creative artists and the society in which they lived. The American Thomas Hart Benton and the Englishman Stanley Spencer were two outstanding products of this remarkable period.

Nowhere was the conflict more evident than in the dream world of the Surrealist movement. This was as much an intellectual movement as an artistic school. The twentieth century first saw a revival of the art of trompe l'oeil murals when the powerful currents in art—Expressionism, Cubism and Dadaism—which had replaced the sensuous colour and light of the Impressionist paintings, were in turn transcended by this new breed of artists. Living in a conservative society which was trying to come to terms with the upheavals foisted upon them by World

War I, the Surrealists were greatly influenced by psychoanalysis, then in its infancy, and by Rimbaud's philosophy that life must be changed by portraying the workings of the subconscious mind.

Using humour and sarcasm, they enjoyed the bizarre juxtaposition of ideas and objects, inducing a sense of unease in the onlooker. Magritte was one of the best interpreters of Surrealist trompe l'oeil, famous for the insertion in his paintings of a third plane of reality. He once said, 'A truly poetic canvas is an awakened dream.' The artist who made Surrealism truly fashionable however, the brilliant and eccentric Salvador Dali, was a latecomer to the movement. Having abandoned the political ideology of his colleagues, he was nicknamed 'Avida Dollars' after captivating America and becoming hugely successful. His passion for money and his reactionary political views infuriated his fellow artists all the more since he persuaded America that he had invented Surrealism singlehanded.

In the midst of this artistic activity, President Franklin Roosevelt initiated a mural programme for out-of-work artists in 1933, under the American New Deal. It was a remarkable act of mass patronage. Besides enabling the artists involved to eat, and helping to reduce the devastating effects of the Depression, the murals also made art accessible to people. The programme was called the Works Progress Administration (WPA), and it commissioned local artists to paint public buildings all over the country. Over a thousand post offices in rural areas were embellished, often, unfortunately, by mediocre paintings. The artists were paid the princely sum of $21 a week.

The period also saw the contemporary mural elevated to an art form again. Thomas Hart Benton and the charismatic Mexican painter Diego Rivera, a contemporary of his fellow countrymen, David Alfaro Siqueiros and José Clemente Orozco—both of whom painted powerful renditions of figurative Modernism—were giants of their time. The murals of Thomas Hart Benton, one of America's favourite artists, often portrayed the economic and social life of the American people; he was foremost among American artists at the time who reacted against the European passion for modern art, believing instead that his own country should become the main subject of native American painting. As he told a critic, 'I wallowed in every cockeyed-ism that came along, and it took me ten years to get all that Modernist dirt out of my system.'

Benton's multi-panelled mural *America Today* (Plate 8) in the Equitable Building in New York draws much of its imagery from his summer sketching trips through the small towns and back roads of America. The jazzy composition of tall figures and small groups depicts realistic scenes of people pursuing their labour and leisure activities in both city and country. Benton derived much of his use of strong light and shade, extreme lighting and grouping from the Italian classicists with many of his distortions coming directly from the Cubists. The mural was originally painted for the New School for Social Research in New York, which was begun in the 1930s as a school for exiles who included artists and scientists and attracted many muralists. Benton's mural was an integral part of the architecture as it had no beginning and no end and filled the whole room, unlike its present site where it is placed on a huge wall for which it was not intended and to which it does not relate.

Thomas Hart Benton, at the time when he was working on this mural, was described in the *Demcourier* by Reginald Marsh.

A little swarthy and cocky man, Benton resembles a well-nourished Sicilian bootblack rather than a midwest oldstock American. When I first got acquainted with him, I called upon him frequently, apparently always in time to help him carry about the studio his 400 lb. murals which he was painting for the New School of Social Research. (I posed for the negro with the drill and learned egg-tempera as a reward.) The time was summer and it was amusing to watch Benton, muscular in his underwear, sit low in an armchair, survey the mural, suddenly load his brush with a lot of tempera goo, crouch like a cat, spring across the room in a flying tackle, scrub the brush around in great circles, catch his breath, and then resume his place in the chair.

9. Rex Whistler. The dining room at Plas Newydd, Wales. 1936–38. Oil on canvas. Lord Anglesey

10. (*overleaf*) Graham Rust. *The Temptation.* 1969–83. Indelible gouache on rag paper. Marquess of Hertford, Ragley Hall, Warwickshire

Benton is a colourful, scrappy, uncouth person, with a demonic energy and a strong tendency to publicize himself. All this is to his credit. If he were to hibernate or vegetate or dress like Fred Astaire, he would be hamstrung undoubtedly. Let him have his flash-bulbs, his harmonicas, his windmills, his mules, his little Pickaninnies and Persephones, it's all part of his constitution.

The themes of social upheaval and class struggle, so prevalent in murals of this period when change, introspection and extremism were recurring themes, are especially reinforced in the work of the Mexican muralist, Diego Rivera. He spent the years of the Mexican revolution in Europe, where he learned the formal lessons of Cubism in Paris, and his return to Mexico in 1921 heralded the true start of his country's prolific mural movement of the 1920s and 1930s.

A large, expansive man, who was affectionately known as Frogface to his friends, he was a champion of the oppressed and painted apocalyptic frescoes on revolutionary themes. Constantly expressing a message of social revolt, he was once described by a contemporary as the 'Raphael of Communism'. Intrigued by his country's history—Mexican art in the pre-Columbian period produced a wealth of mural painting—Rivera also had a deep affection for Mexico's Indians and their pre-Hispanic past. He had also been fascinated by machinery since he was a boy. Both were to appear in complex designs and vibrant colour in his murals. Rivera's frescoes filled with people were executed with immense creative vigour, and his portrayals of American industrial environments such as Detroit were rendered with great feeling for, and accurate depiction of, machinery.

Rivera was a womanizer, a great raconteur and compulsive liar. He looked grotesque and was outrageously eccentric. His greatest love, however, was mural painting and he dedicated his life to it. His second wife, Frida Kahlo, said of him:

No words can describe the immense tenderness of Diego for the things that had beauty. . . . He especially loves the Indians, for their elegance, their beauty, and because they are the living flower of the cultural tradition of America. He loves children, all animals . . . and birds, plants and stones. His diversion is his work . . . his capacity for work breaks clocks and calendars. He tries to do and has done what he considers just in life: to work and create. . . .

In Europe, despite the persecution of artists in some countries which forced them into exile, there were some major achievements. Paris, which was widely regarded as the centre of the visual arts during the 1930s, fittingly housed the greatest mural of its time: Picasso's masterpiece, *Guernica*, was created for the Spanish pavilion at the Paris Exposition Universelle of 1937. Employing powerful symbolism of Spanish culture and his favourite images of the weeping woman and the dying horse, Picasso evoked the tragedy of his native Spain being torn apart by civil war.

While foreign artists from many different countries settled in Paris, the 1930s in England, as in America, was a period of creative activity. England has never been in the forefront of mural activity, partly because of its unfavourable climate, and much of the best work was carried out by imported Italian artists. Also, unlike America and Mexico, murals in England did not have the impetus of political and social upheavals behind them.

There were, nevertheless, a number of muralists, other than the popular decorative artist Rex Whistler and the powerful figurative painter Stanley Spencer, who were well versed in the art. The best known and most prolific, although considered by many critics today to be overrated, were Duncan Grant and Vanessa Bell, two prominent members of the Bloomsbury group. Vanessa Bell was the writer Virginia Woolf's sister, and she often worked in conjunction with Duncan Grant whose work was spontaneous and unconstrained, full of bright, rich colour. He also

had a great flair for decorative designs. His involvement with the Omega workshop, founded by the critic and painter Roger Fry, produced works of unexpected originality in his designs for carpets, marquetry and needlework. Both Grant and Bell, as well as the eclectic artist Edward Wadsworth, designed mural panels for the *Queen Mary*, although, much to Grant's chagrin, his panels for the new liner were rejected.

One of the most important murals of the period was Stanley Spencer's painting in the Oratory of All Souls, Burghclere, near Newbury, which he worked on for five years between 1927 and 1932. The theme for this war memorial was based on his experiences during the Great War, when he served with the army in Macedonia. Spencer, an English eccentric, had the rare distinction of being employed both as soldier and war artist in both World Wars. His paintings on the subject provide a lasting and valuable insight into war. Rather than dwell on the horrors of battle, the mural cycle depicts the human comradeship and closeness attained during the dark days of war. On hearing that Mr and Mrs J.L. Behrend had decided to build a chapel especially to house his ambitious mural design, Spencer's crisp reaction was 'What ho, Giotto!' This was a reference to the Italian master's decoration of the Arena chapel in Padua, with which Spencer's mural arrangement has much in common.

A masterpiece full of exuberance, the mural was painted in oil on huge seamless canvases woven in Belgium. As the visitor steps through the front door of the small chapel, he is almost overwhelmed by its crowded movement. The two side walls are filled with the rounded and curiously doll-like figures of soldiers, engaged in the humdrum pursuits of military routine. No glory here, for the unfortunate foot soldier, just kit inspection, a convoy arriving with the wounded, scrubbing the hospital floor, dressing and shaving under mosquito nets. Dominating this pedantic scene is the theme of the main wall, the 'Resurrection of the Soldiers'. A mass of white wooden crosses, clutched by the awakened soldiers, fills the wall. Christ, who is seen in the middle distance receives them. The picture conveys a powerful message about the relationship between war, death and Christianity.

A number of other artists in England at the time were experimenting with murals, among them Eric Ravilious, Tristram Hillier, Hans Feibusch, Edward Bawden and Mary Adshead. The last three were still painting in the 1980s, although, being themselves in their eighties, they had given up the rigours of the scaffold.

Mary Adshead was a student with Rex Whistler at the Slade School of Art in the mid-1920s under the legendary Professor Henry Tonks. She reminisces: 'Tonks used to be quite beastly to all the girl students in the beginning. But by the time I got there he had softened and was very fatherly towards me. He always made a great effort to get jobs for people in whom he had faith after they left the Slade. Thank God he started me on murals with Rex Whistler, otherwise the Slade would not have been any use to me at all.'

Lord Beaverbrook commissioned a number of panels from Mary Adshead for the dining-room walls of Calvin House. He wanted a number of his own friends wandering around the painting. In one panel Lady Diana Cooper can be seen enjoying a *déjeuner sur l'herbe* with some admirers (Plate 7). In another the Aga Khan is smiling broadly at Lord Derby as he brings in the winner at the Newmarket races (Plate 6). Unfortunately the mural panels were never used. Lady Diana, who was having a passionate affair with Lord Beaverbrook at the time, told him that as soon as the mural was up on the wall he would have quarrelled with all his friends in the picture and not want them around. The rolled-up canvases were found in 1985 in Mary Adshead's attic, having been completely forgotten for over fifty years.

The reputation of Rex Whistler as a decorative artist was firmly established when, at the age of twenty and just having finished studying at the Slade, he was commissioned by Lord Duveen to paint a mural in the Tate Gallery restaurant. Taking into account its placing, Whistler chose the humorous theme of 'The Pursuit of Rare Meats', from an Arcadian strip cartoon. Gaily clad men and women set out on an expedition through romantic scenery in search of delicious varieties of food.

Whistler, a sensitive and slightly dreamy young man, was a remarkably versatile artist. Besides murals, he drew bookplates, illustrated novels and volumes of poems, designed for the theatre and executed easel painting and portraiture. He had a rich imagination and an admiration for eighteenth-century architecture, which found expression in his most important mural at Plas Newydd in Wales, painted in 1936 (Plate 9). Built by the father of 'One Leg', one of England's finest cavalry commanders who was made marquess of Anglesey after the battle of Waterloo, Plas Newydd was then the home of the sixth marquess.

The long wall of the dining room was transformed into an elegant Baroque loggia with an idealized romantic landscape of a harbour dotted with sailing vessels and surrounded by mountain ranges. Fishing tackle is left littering the jetty, which has a mysterious wet footprint on the pavement. In front of these a trident rests nonchalantly against an urn, giving one the humorous notion that perhaps Neptune has risen from the depths of the sea and gone into the house. One of the two colonnades at either end of the room shows Whistler, the gardener, holding a broom.

The outbreak of war in 1939 interrupted artistic life over most of Europe. Rex Whistler, whose reputation as a decorative artist has survived, died in battle in 1944. In the worsening economic climate the commissioning of murals became an unnecessary frivolity. A few artists quietly worked away at producing, for the most part unheralded, work in the 1950s. It was not until the 1960s that the desire to embellish buildings with wallpaintings again became fashionable.

11. Graham Rust. *The Temptation*. 1969–83. Indelible gouache on rag paper. Marquess of Hertford, Ragley Hall, Warwickshire

12. Ian Cairnie. 1986. Oil, 475 × 317 cm (180 × 120 in). Mrs Sheila Oakes

MURALS IN THE GRAND MANNER

At the end of a long, winding drive, deep in the Warwickshire countryside and surrounded on both sides by sheep nibbling on acres of green grass, lies Ragley Hall, the imposing house of the marquess and marchioness of Hertford. After its wartime use as a hospital, the early Palladian house, originally built in 1680, was almost derelict, and was then lovingly restored by the family. It is one of the finest examples of a Baroque interior in England, with 115 rooms laid out symmetrically from the Great Hall. This seventeenth-century stately home contains what is probably the most important contemporary mural done in Britain, possibly anywhere. This outstanding wallpainting is the work of Graham Rust, England's most celebrated contemporary muralist (Plates 2, 10, 11, 13). The visitor comes across the vast mural having first passed through the Great Hall with its intricate white plaster decorations against pale pink walls designed in 1750 by James Gibbs. The mural is 40 feet high and the ceiling mural is 40 feet long, claiming the title of the largest mural painted in a private house this century. Rex Whistler, although so prolific, completed no commissions comparable in size to this work.

Graham Rust's mural can be loosely termed a mural painted in the 'Grand Manner'. This definition encompasses murals whose conception is based on the great eras of classical painting and architecture of the past. Many contemporary murals contain a large element of nostalgia but the current revival of interest in classical and Gothic painting, the sumptuous style and the masterly technique of many of these contemporary artists' creative powers go beyond the merely decorative. As the artist Francis Bacon says, 'The job of the artist is always to deepen the mystery.'

Murals painted in this manner are often commissioned for large, historically important houses, such as Ragley Hall, to create the illusion and reality of permanence—the house built three hundred years ago shows faith in its future by commissioning a mural on a grand scale. Such murals are meant to last. Important examples of this kind are often painted in the period in which the house was built.

Graham Rust, a charming and self-effacing artist, spent an average of one week a month from 1969 to 1983 painting a modern version of *The Temptation*. The theme was chosen by Lord Hertford, after climbing to the

13. Graham Rust. *The Temptation* ceiling. 1969–83. Indelible gouache on rag paper. Marquess of Hertford, Ragley Hall

14. Richard Shirley Smith. 1976. Acrylic, 380 × 253 cm (144 × 96 in). Private collection

top of the Mount of Temptation, in Israel, in 1952. He spent a cold few days posing as a semi-clad and shivering Neptune for the huge mural when Rust was in dire need of a model, although the experience had its lighter moments.

The romantic colouring and highly imaginative design were inspired by Rust's admiration for the sixteenth-century Italian painter, Paolo Veronese, especially for those frescoes at the Villa Barbero, built by Andrea Palladio at Maser. Against a pale background of imaginary landscapes, follies, and forty-two marble columns, complete with hybrid tops, splashes of dramatic colour stand out: two scarlet ibis, a nonchalant cheetah tied to a column by a gilded chain and wearing round its neck a red collar complete with an emerald clasp copied from Lady Hertford's emerald tiara. Rust's favourite natural subjects—flowers, birds, shells, animals, plants and trees, within a strong architectural framework—fill the lower walls. A bright pink spoonbill catches the eye; toucans perch on architectural plinths and dolphins' heads; a colubus monkey sits and stares out from the base of a palm tree; ripened fruit spills out from a cornucopia; cherubs chase each other round a beehive. The gaiety and the colourful objects portrayed in minute and loving detail lie in rich harmony with the centre pieces of these two walls: two painted marble statues of Bernini's *Neptune and Triton* on one side and *Samson and a Philistine* by Giambologna on the other.

As in murals painted in the sixteenth century, such as Veronese's fresco in the Stanza dell'Olimpo at the Villa Barbero, life-size figures are included, in this case of the family, their friends and servants. Lord and Lady Hertford, together with their four children and their children's godparents, stand on the top balcony with its vivid coat of arms. Surprisingly, given Rust's masterly draughtsmanship and sense of composition, the figures are the least successful part of the mural. They appear slightly stilted in their modern dress.

Rust has been painting murals for twenty years. He likes his murals to appeal on different levels, especially at Ragley Hall which is on permanent show to the public. He has fulfilled his desire to impart a sweeping grandeur in this mural, but with enough to interest the eye in the smaller details. It is that balance which gives the wallpainting its overall feeling of harmony.

Baroque art's speciality was the creation of movement in space and from there into infinity. The incessant use of ascending architecture, painted with its numerous galleries and pillars, flying saints and cherubs floating through billowing clouds, produced in the spectator a feeling of drifting into a fantastic dream world. This feeling of heavenly space is the climax of the mural at Ragley Hall in the vast ceiling painting. The *Temptation of Christ* is painted in an open dome with the false perspective of the architectural walls bringing to the room an even greater feeling of height. While the Devil, resplendent in roseate robes, offers Christ the world with all its riches, symbolized by a circle of gold, the humorous figures of the family butler and cook peer down from the balcony onto the scene below.

A ceiling is by far the most daunting physical task for a muralist. The energy needed to stand for hours with an outstretched arm above the head is a great challenge. It is essential to get the working drawing for the ceiling accurate, since the artist, being only at arm's length and perched on scaffolding, cannot see the whole. Many of the most spectacular European works of art in the past were achieved in close partnership between commissioned artists and their patron. With scaffolding continually present and the artist working over an undetermined length of time, the relationship between Lord Hertford and Graham Rust is a rare contemporary example of mutual understanding and patience, imagination and technique, evolving into a major work of art.

Although the idiosyncracies of each muralist, their experience and their use of paint underline their individuality, the techniques of painting a successful mural follow a well-rehearsed path. A muralist should see the room which he is to decorate. Just as an architect cannot complete his design for a building without seeing the site, the muralist needs to study the proportions of the room, where the light comes from and the architecture which the mural is to enhance. Each room is unique, and although many artists prefer working unhampered in the studio if the mural is on canvas or panels, it is preferable to work on site where they can get the feel of the surroundings and also adjust the depth of the paint and colour tone.

After completing a maquette—a detailed painted sketch or preliminary model—usually done to one-tenth of the proposed size of the mural, the artist scales up his design onto the wall, canvas or wooden panel. Scaling up is done in various ways. This can be done freehand, using a number of marked guide lines in a grid pattern in which each of the squares represents the smaller square in the original drawing, or the finished sketch can be photographed and projected up onto the wall or canvas. Some painters are driven to distraction by such tedious preparations and draw directly onto the wall, ticking off crucial places to guide them. Occasionally a cartoon of the proposed mural is traced onto the wall.

The design is drawn on in charcoal, chalk or pencil. The outline is then drawn over in red ochre or sepia. Before beginning to paint, some muralists prefer to cover the whole area in a basic monochrome to get a rough balance for the tone, rather than the colour. The most important technique in mural painting is for the tone to be right for the atmosphere of the room. There is no definitive way of applying paint and glazes and every muralist

16. Sarah Janson. *Pompeii*. 1984. Oil, 634 × 317 cm (240 × 120 in). Mr and Mrs Michael Astor

15. (*previous page*) Felix Kelly. Oil on canvas, 412 × 158 × 127 cm (156 × 60 × 48 in). Castle Howard collection, Yorkshire

has his own approach when painting a mural. Usually the mid-tones of the painting are blocked out, followed by the darker and lighter tones. Only when the larger colour areas are painted in evenly, can the artist then concentrate on the smaller details of his mural.

The cost of murals depends on the talent and relative fame of the artist. Some charge a few hundred pounds, some a few thousand and the elite a small fortune. In 1986 a Texan executive paid $250,000 for a mural measuring 24 feet by 8 feet. The price depends partly on the length of time taken to complete the work, the size of the wall and the complexity of the design. Graham Rust spent five months intricately painting an historical theme on the ceiling of a chapel in Virginia which had been especially designed to house a mural. The average-sized mural takes about four weeks to complete at an approximate price of £4,800 in England and $20,000 in America, although the best-known muralists in both countries command a great deal more. This may seem expensive but the pleasure derived from a fine mural is worth every penny.

'Grand Manner' murals are almost by definition traditional in their composition and richness of detail. Like their predecessors they often take many months or even years to complete, as shown in the case of the thirteen-year commission at Ragley Hall. Traditional motifs used throughout the classical ages continually appear in contemporary 'Grand Manner' murals. The most prolific is theatrical architecture, including flights of steps, painted moulded enrichments, acanthus leaves, shells and columns and pilasters with elaborate capitals, reminiscent of Agostino Tassi's grandiose fresco in the Palazzo Lancellotti ai Coronari, Rome (1617–23). Another favoured motif at that time, which continues to thrive today, was exotic birds, the symbol of wealth, luxury and taste. The lapis lazuli colours of a strutting peacock or the scarlet ibis painted at Ragley Hall all add a sense of enchantment to a painting.

Painted statues in classical costume, such as those painted by Veronese in the room of the Tribunal of Love, at the Villa Barbero (c.1560), are a popular modern motif. These statues and niches are still often painted in grisaille as imitations of sculpture. The word 'grisaille' comes from the French word 'gris' and means to paint in various tones of grey. In the fifteenth century Masaccio and Mantegna were keen exponents of this particular art, and Jan van Eyck's picture of statues painted in grisaille, *The Annunciation* (c.1434) at the Galleria Thyssen, Lugano, Italy, is a perfect example of the genre. In the late eighteenth century, the plump figures of putti became a well-liked subject for grisaille painting.

A favourite motif in the past was the dwarf, used in paintings as a foil to the beautiful and sumptuously dressed upper classes. Tiepolo depicted them in various ways—grimacing, in his fresco in the Palazzo Clerici, Milan (c.1740), or as a fawning courtier in the Palazzo Labia (c.1746). Other distinctive features common to grand traditional murals past and present are cherubs and colourful garlands of flowers, urns, nature and ruins, all of which were beautifully portrayed by Giovanni Francesco Grimaldi in his sumptuous fresco in the Hall of Spring, Villa Falconieri, Rome, in 1672. The cartouche (a small scroll-like ornamentation) and the cartellino have been a part of mural painting since the Renaissance. A cartellino is a curled-up slip of paper, integrated into the painting, which bears the artist's signature.

Expressing themselves in a contemporary language, muralists today look towards the past for their inspiration, especially towards Italy and France. Their greatest inspiration tends to come from the grandeur and excesses of the Baroque and especially from the frescoes of Giambattista Tiepolo, commissioned for palaces, churches and villas. Tiepolo was the last in the line of the great Venetian mural painters, and he had an extraordinary grasp of the technique of fresco painting. His absolute mastery of colour, draughtsmanship and the seemingly effortless airiness and lightness of his painted visions, are among the highlights of Baroque art. He imbued his frescoes with a combination of gravity and gaiety, a constant feeling of dramatic excitement and

19. Evergreene Studios. 1986. Acrylic on linen, 380 × 222 cm (144 × 84 in). Millie's Place Restaurant

festivity. The greatest example of his work, on the colossal staircase ceiling of the episcopal palace at Würzburg, centres on a radiant Apollo as sun god, dominating the earth, with allegories of the four continents filled with people in exquisite costumes, rare plants and exotic beasts.

At a time when most of the great murals were concentrated in Italy, late-seventeenth-century England was slowly emerging from a period when the development of the arts had been warped by the puritan influence. There were few excellent British artists able to decorate the houses of the upper classes. The only decorative, but second-rate, artist in the Baroque style was James Thornhill (1675–1734), father-in-law of Hogarth. Apart from his huge commission at Greenwich Hospital, he painted the dome of Christopher Wren's St Paul's Cathedral and a large ceiling mural in Queen Anne's bedroom at Hampton Court.

An important source of murals in English houses at the time was the Grand Tour, undertaken by the young and wealthy who travelled round Europe and especially Italy with its much-admired artistic heritage. When commissioning murals for their grand houses, they preferred to import Italian artists who were more skilled than the local variety, as a way of displaying their recently acquired taste in the arts. Among the main exponents of foreign talent working in England were the Italian painters Antonio Verrio, who belonged to the French Academy, Antonio Pellegrini and Sebastiano Ricci. All three were in great demand, and Verrio painted murals for the aristocracy at Windsor Castle, Chatsworth, Hampton Court and Burghley House. Claude Lorrain and Louis Laguerre were other foreign painters actively enhancing the grandeur of domestic architecture, but none of the murals painted then could rival the sumptuous standards reached by the Baroque and Rococo artists in Italy.

One of Pellegrini's mural commissions was for Lord Carlisle's Castle Howard in Yorkshire. This was the first great house to be built by the architect Sir John Vanbrugh, in 1699. The destruction by fire in 1940 of

20. Owen Turville. 1975. Oil, 634 × 317 cm (240 × 120 in). Private collection

Pellegrini's murals, along with paintings by Tintoretto, Reynolds and Canaletto, tragic though this may have been, provided the opportunity for the commissioning of a new set of magnificent murals (Plate 15) by the well-known contemporary painter Felix Kelly, a New Zealander who has made England his home for the past fifty years. The house was used in the television series *Brideshead Revisited*, the dramatization of Evelyn Waugh's novel, and the late Lord Howard, owner of the house, was able to realize his long-cherished dream of creating a garden room in the spirit of Vanbrugh. In the television dramatization, the fictional character Charles Ryder needed a room in which he could practise his love of decorative wallpainting. Lord Howard called upon his old friend Felix Kelly, whose paintings are among the most sought after in Europe. Kelly filled four niches in the garden room with mysterious dreamlike landscapes. Moss-covered trees, deep soul-stirring waters and dancing shafts of light surround the central theme of imaginary buildings which are much in the same vein as those Vanbrugh might have built.

Kelly's dark, haunting paintings combine romanticism with the melancholy beauty associated with a grander, forgotten age. Even the well-informed can be fooled by his Castle Howard murals. 'Soon after the room was opened by the Queen Mother', says Kelly, 'I got a letter from a well-known architectural scholar, writing that he could not find these buildings in any of his reference books on Vanbrugh and would I tell him where I had found them.'

An essentially romantic painter with a profound love and knowledge of architecture, especially Gothick, Kelly does not rate painting murals as his favourite occupation. Like many other muralists he enjoys the challenge of working out his ideas and completing the maquette best, but finds the actual wallpainting tedious. He says, 'It's like having a love affair again with someone once it is over.'

Although most contemporary muralists have no illusions about surpassing the heights achieved by the Italian masters in portraying architecture, it still remains their favourite subject in a mural. Apart from the accurate architectural knowledge and perspective needed to achieve any degree of realism, the solid lines of stone masonry can be softened by the inclusion of nature.

The idea of luxuriant gardens seemingly invading rooms has been part of the muralists' creative vocabulary since the days of the Romans. A delightful example was a fresco painted in the first century BC, probably by the artist Studius Ludius, for the garden room in the house of Livia, wife of Emperor Augustus. Here, the brilliant colour which was common to Roman frescoes spills across the walls in the form of a garden full of small birds flitting among flowering oleander plants and cypress trees.

A small London garden reverses the illusion of interior walls covered in an ornate fantasy of foliage. Here the foliage is real and the architecture is fake. The wall at the end of Roy Alderson's private garden is an extension of his inventive house in London's Chelsea, every room of which includes a mural (Plate 1). Even when standing in the small romantic garden, a few feet away from the mural, the grand flight of stone steps leading up to a rose-covered balustrade appears real. But the balustrade and fantastic urns are wooden cutouts shaded to suggest the roundness and solidity of stone. Balustrades and urns have always been a popular motif to include in a mural, with a perfect example being those painted by Angelo Michele Colonna and Agostino Mitelli in the Palazzo Pitti, Florence, between 1636 and 1641. A feeling of permanent sunshine pervades Alderson's garden, caused by the strong painted shadow on the steps. The only piece of reality in this theatrical setting besides the dense greenery is the shapely terracotta statue of a woman, deliberately painted a dirty colour to tone in with the rest of the illusion.

The Romantic penchant for a decaying world of classical ruins enveloped by nature has never really left us. The English artist Tony Raymond has exploited this to transform a tiny stairwell in a north London home into a spacious ruined vista (Plate 18). Raymond observes, 'If you paint a column or a piece of stonework, you must

21. Felix Kelly. *The Endeavour*. 1985. Oil on board, 127 × 190 cm (48 × 72 in). On Mr Tommy Sopwith's yacht

create the texture and solidity of stone. I like to go one step further and spend hours painting a few butterflies with their shadows, or a bumble bee.' This mural is painted in Flashe, French emulsion paints that were originally developed for restoration work, and which fuse into the plaster when dry. Down the stairs from the dining room, a well-fed parrot clutches a grape in its beak. Lying in front on silken draperies, one of Raymond's trompe l'oeil specialities, are the residues of a good meal—a flagon of wine, crystal goblets and a bowl of tempting fruit. With clever perspective and gentle colours of stone, pale greens and greys, enfolding the spectator, the structural solidity of the narrow passage is removed and the eye gazes out onto the ravages of time stretching to seemingly endless horizons.

Love of nature is also to be found in simulated tapestries which often have a background of plants and trees. Although popular as an art form in the sixteenth and seventeenth centuries, tapestries were previously painted to decorate early Christian churches. A lively example of simulated tapestry was the fresco by Baldassare Croce (1558–1628), *Susanna and the Elders*, in the church of Santa Susanna, Rome. Tapestries were also painted when the real object was too costly. The art is to make the painting have the feel and the look of tapestry. This is usually achieved by painting on canvas, linen, or vinyl with a canvas texture. The simulated tapestry is painted tightly with flat colours with the hatching always going down and not across, in imitation of the weave. The colours of successful tapestry painting are very distinctive with the softer greens for ageing foliage and muted colours for statuary and architecture.

The tapestry designed by Jeff Greene, of Evergreene Studios in Manhattan, stretches across a wall of a restaurant in Long Island (Plate 19). A compilation of elements from the famed Unicorn Tapestry in France, the mural is based on the William Morris style. It was done on rough linen in diluted Flashe paint, spread very lightly over the whole surface so that the heavy weave of the linen comes through like tapestry. Connotations of fecundity and virility spring out from the painting—the serpent, the satyr and the crow on the woman's left shoulder all leave visions of the darker corners of temptation in the viewer's imagination.

The addition of the human figure in contemporary murals has always been controversial. Unless the draughtsmanship is excellent, their appearance looks static—possibly because we are used to seeing people in motion—and upsets the balance and rhythm of the painting. One painter whose exotic mural figures combine a lucidity of form with a looseness of style is the Los Angeles-based muralist Douglas Riseborough. He has been perfecting his craft for the past forty years. His large colourful mural *Memory of Marrakesh*, which was commissioned soon after a visit by the artist to Morocco, is peopled with richly painted North Africans (Plate 23). The work is so realistic that figures appear to be standing in the drawing room. This clever trompe l'oeil effect is achieved by the addition of a dilapidated wall to the composition, the same height as the fireplace. In front of this two figures invade the spectator's space, while another nonchalantly leans over the wall, airing a rug. The earth tones, which are often used by Riseborough, blend in with the browns and russets of the furniture and floor. The overall effect is both theatrical and homogenous.

Contemporary renditions of Pompeiian and Baroque themes are to be found in homes basking in the warm Californian climate. Like Italy, the natural home of the mural, California is light, warm and a perfect setting for murals. It also has a special interest in funding public art, as well as the money, the buildings and the growing talent to produce the most exciting murals of the future.

In a large elegant yellow house overlooking San Francisco Bay, the prolific Californian muralist Garth Benton, cousin of Thomas Hart Benton, has interpreted romantic Italian life in the style of Tiepolo for his client, Mrs Ann Getty (Plates 4, 22). The downstairs of the house is dominated by a vast atrium surrounded by marble pilasters and highlighted by a black and white marble floor. In all four corners of the atrium and along one entire wall of the courtyard dramatic swags of painted silken green and white drapes are swept back, revealing scenes of eighteenth-century courtly life—a sumptuously dressed woman parading beneath a romantic yellow parasol, the classical motif of a dwarf playing with a monkey, turbaned Nubians and dogs. The sun shining through the roof playfully lengthens the painted shadows, blurring the boundaries between reality and illusion.

The opulence and drama of the eighteenth century, so richly depicted by Tiepolo, was to have another lasting effect on muralists of today. The small mischievous figures of the Commedia dell'Arte characters, particularly as depicted by Giambattista's son, Domenico, in his Pulchinella drawings and murals in his villa on the Veneto in Italy, are frequent sources of inspiration. Comic or bizarre figures and fantastic beasts in murals are fun and create the illusion of a lighthearted world without boundaries, full of childhood dreams peopled with goblins and fairies and ribald Pulchinellas. Among the earliest renditions of figures from the Commedia dell'Arte were the murals in Trausnitz castle in the Bavarian town of Landshut, painted in 1578 by the Dutch artist Friedrich Sustris and his brother-in-law Alessandro Scalzi for Wilhelm V of Wittelsbach.

Similar exuberant puckish creatures figure prominently in the highly original murals and paintings of Richard Shirley Smith. This wry and quietly humorous artist has a special fondness for the Commedia dell'Arte

22. Garth Benton. 1986. Acrylic, 4·75 × 12·67 m (15 × 40 ft). Mrs Ann Getty

23. Douglas Riseborough. *Memory of Marrakesh*.
Acrylic, 887 × 444 cm (336 × 168 in).
Mr William Chidester

24. Richard Shirley
    Smith. 1985.
    Acrylic,
    285 × 634 cm
    (108 × 240 in).
    Lady Brunner

25. Roy Alderson. 1980. Oil, 507 × 158 cm (192 × 60 in). Artist's collection

26. Lincoln Taber. 1968. Tempera, 475 × 475 cm (180 × 180 in). Private collection

27. Richard Haas. 1977. Acrylic, 317 × 380 cm (120 × 144 in). Nancy Rosen and Michael Blackwood

characters. But he draws his greatest inspiration from the architecture of the Veneto in Italy. 'I was also greatly influenced by the magnificent buildings and sculptures in the countryside around Verona,' he says. 'They were in every stage of romantic decay heightened by the bright Italian sun and projected shadow. Great ballrooms had become barns and rustic rakes leaned on the busts of the Caesars.'

Richard Shirley Smith has an exceptional eye for detail and lighting. His work often reflects a strong appeal to the senses—lemons for taste, a woman's breast for touch, stone architecture for strength. His murals, all of which contain an element of trompe l'oeil, possess a uniformity of colour and mood with subtle muted stone tones. They often depict bizarre subject matter set against classical architecture or details of architectural drawings by Piranesi, whom Shirley Smith especially admires for his skill and lively imagination. Infinitely detailed shells and roots, crabs and puppets, disembodied dolls' legs and fossils enhance the feel of surrealism.

Richard Shirley Smith's work also stresses the sinister and broken things of life, the cruel thought. 'I think sentimentality and chocolate-box niceties are an idiocy in art and a total misrepresentation of life. I have to have the small shadows behind in my work if it is to be at all related to real life.' Apart from the challenge of working on a large scale, one of the reasons he loves doing murals around an entire room is the feeling of 'being cocooned inside a painted box'—a three-dimensional space which gives a completion to his work. His work is much in demand, but he feels dubious about publicity. 'The only query I got from doing Lady Brunner's publicized mural was which shop did the teacups in the picture come from' (Plate 24).

His five panels owned by Clayform Properties in London combine many of his unique elements (Plate 28). Torn paper covered with architectural drawings of a church apse, an Ionic capital, a patterned paper used on the back of playing cards, is ripped open to reveal a tranquil world of fruit and a villa on the Veneto. Shirley Smith got the idea of using torn paper from the illuminated books of the Renaissance. He enjoys the rich quilted quality it gives as it gradates around its curvature. Shadows are thrown across the painting where the paper casts its reflected lights, especially where it is folded up like a map. It is easy to tear the paper when it is repeating itself or when it starts to become less interesting, enabling pieces of architecture or still life to disappear behind it. Fluttering ribbons of gossamer, one holding a snake copied from a family emblem belonging to the duke and duchess of Devonshire at Chatsworth, and the addition of delicately coloured butterflies all add to the feel of lightness.

All Richard Shirley Smith's murals are worked on a chiaroscuro basis, with the strong use of contrasting light and shade and always with a sideways rake of light coming into his pictures. He often photographs the elements that go into his paintings. He says, 'Whenever I see anything which has escaped from my work, I capture it on camera and take it home and put it back where it belongs.' He then traces the projected photograph onto the wall, changing the image here and there to make it unique.

On the other side of the Atlantic, classical Italy is again a source of inspiration. Carlos Marchiori's green clapboard house in San Francisco, with a large tiger painted across the front, houses a contemporary rendition of a purely illusionist Roman mural (Plate 31). Steeped in love for his native Italy and the rich roots of his birthplace, Venice, Marchiori's murals are traditionally inspired. He no longer accepts any commissions from prospective American clients, which he considers to be 'architectural indigestion' or 'Tiepolo revisited'.

His bedroom is an inventive interpretation of a decaying Roman room. Using the deep reds and dark tones reminiscent of the mural in the house of Lucrezio Frontone in Pompeii, dating from the first century BC, he calls it 'Pompeiiana'. After leaving on the original dun-coloured wallpaper, ordinary housepaint was used to achieve the subtle fresco-like colouring used by the ancients. The only part of the wall which was not painted freehand was the figurative artwork which was stencilled. Marchiori then quickly and deliberately 'destroys' his

28. Richard Shirley Smith. 1984. Acrylic, five 190 × 127 cm (72 × 48 in) panels. Clayform Properties Ltd, London

29. Felix Kelly. *Tuscaloosa River Scene*. Oil on board, 127 × 190 cm (48 × 60 in). Jack W. Warner

walls with sandpaper. 'Impatience is my best quality', he stresses. Pieces of paper covered with white paint are then rolled onto the wall in various places to imply the feel and look of wear and tear, and grey paint is spattered onto the mural to suggest mould. This method, together with the blocking out and scraping away of entire chunks of painted surface, results in one third of the original painting disappearing, producing a highly original interpretation of an authentic Roman villa.

Two vastly different compositions portraying the human figure reside in an English stately home and a London restaurant. London-based Ricardo Cinalli treats the grandeur of the past in a totally contemporary way. Set against the crisp white architecture of the Braganza Restaurant, his recurring theme of the fragmented body appears as magnified pieces of broken sculpture surrounded by fallen marble pillars (Plate 32).

One of the best examples of painterly knowledge combined with simplicity of design is the work commissioned by the Duke of Wellington's son from the well-known British portrait painter and muralist Howard Morgan (Plate 33). A dramatic painter, Morgan stresses that 'The English don't on the whole produce large-scale painters who do strong, powerful painting—theirs is not the art of princes.' Irritated by continually being compared to Sargent, Morgan says, 'One of the reasons I am different to Sargent is precisely because he had no imaginative capacity or talent for painting murals. I don't paint the same kinds of things as he did, nor are my preoccupations the same. I am concerned with a lot of the things European painters are preoccupied with—the allegory, the solitary, religious pictures. My influences are the European thoroughbreds which go right back to Tiepolo, and my passion, Masaccio.'

Morgan decided to paint a flat mural around his client's long narrow dining room and to keep the long wall relatively empty in order not to oppress and narrow the room even further. A flat mural is one whose main movement and rhythm runs along the wall, with no depth, therefore not breaking into it. On one wall the beautiful young mistress of the house, who is a superb organizer and horsewoman, is portrayed wearing a hunting outfit and carrying a whip, symbol of both her efficiency and equestrian ability. A rag doll sitting on the balustrade represents her childlike side. The waiter, who is walking the other way, does a double take as she walks out of the room, having just set up a seemingly effortless dinner party. On the opposite wall troubadours are serenading the guests with dreadful voices while the real musicians are resting. The strength of the figure drawing and richly luminous use of paint by the artist give the mural a tremendous sense of freedom and excitement.

30. (*previous page*) Alan
    Dodd. 1981–82.
    Oil, 444 × 634 cm
    (168 × 240 in).
    Private collection

31. Carlos Marchiori.
    1986. Emulsion,
    475 × 475 cm
    (180 × 180 in).
    Artist's collection

33. Howard Morgan. 1982. Casein, 792 × 380 cm (300 × 144 in). Private collection

32. Ricardo Cinalli. 1986. Oil on board and wall, 600 × 500 cm (227 × 189 in). Braganza Restaurant, Soho, London

34. Lincoln Taber. *Beaters' Lodge.* 1978. Tempera, 475 × 317 cm (180 × 120 in). John Joliffe-Tufnell

35. Richard Haas. 1976. Acrylic, 4·12 × 4·75 × 10·14 m (13 × 15 × 32 ft). Mr and Mrs Peter Nelson

36. Christian Thee. 1975. Acrylic on wood, 190 × 79 cm (72 × 30 in). Flint Institute of Art, Flint, Michigan

37. Christian Thee. *Rebecca's Wing* (after Daphne du Maurier's book). 1972. Acrylic on wood, 174 × 95 cm (66 × 36 in). Private collection

TROMPE L'OEIL MURALS

According to legend, Giotto, while still an apprentice in Cimabue's workshop in thirteenth-century Florence, painted a fly on the nose of a portrait. The deception was so realistic that his master tried to brush it away. For Giotto, this witty trompe l'oeil was just a good-humoured prank but today this kind of artistic deception is an earnest pursuit and big business.

Literally translated, trompe l'oeil means to 'deceive the eye'. For a split second, sometimes longer, the onlooker is fooled into believing that what he sees is real. Surprise is the vital element and the technique requires great skill and the consummate use of perspective. The first recorded example of this form of wallpainting is mentioned by the Roman author Pliny the Elder. More than two thousand years ago in Athens, the painter Zeuxis produced a painting of grapes so realistic that birds flew up to peck at them.

A trompe l'oeil panel is very personal and has a 'small is beautiful' intimacy about it. It feeds an almost universal desire to escape into a world where fantasy invades the senses. It needs very little space and, compared to a large wallpainting, is more affordable. Trompe l'oeil are also less intimidating and obtrusive to live with than a vast mural. On the other hand, by its nature, it tends to be a contrived rather than a passionate art form. The best trompe l'oeil murals go beyond visual deception and they unfold their secrets slowly as the inner eye adjusts from surprise to confusion. This is usually followed by a disappointing adjustment to reality—the grapes are not real after all—and, finally, delight at the skill of this visual confidence trick.

One of the modern masters of the art is the American Christian Thee. His world is a magical place both in the literal and the metaphorical sense. Thee is a prize-winning magician of the rabbit-out-of-a-hat variety, a stage designer, as well as a renowned exponent of trompe l'oeil. This ebullient and enthusiastic man imbues his audience with a sense of being caught up in his fantasies. He says that all his murals stem from his interest in designing for the theatre. Many of his smaller trompe l'oeil works are constructions—painted screens and shutters, window frames surrounding a mysterious figure or an intricate scene, painted on gessoed wood. Gesso is a fine plaster, bound with glue size, which builds up a hard surface on which the paint is then applied.

Thee has always had the ambition to incorporate magic in a painting. One of his most effective works is now owned by the Flint Institute of Art, Michigan (Plate 36). He calls it 'magic realism'. People looking at it revert to being children because they simply cannot figure out how it works. At first they see a painted window covered by a pair of real shutters which are fixed to a wooden panel. When the shutters are pulled back, they reveal a predatory cat on a windowsill eyeing a caged canary. When the shutters are closed and reopened, the canary and the cat have changed places. The castles in the sky have metamorphosed into clouds and the artist's name, or cartellino, which had been partly torn away, has been reinstated. The device is cleverly constructed with electronic magnets on the surface of one shutter and the canvas, but it would give the game away to reveal the complicated trickery involved and would spoil the illusion for future visitors to the Institute. This small trompe l'oeil is an ingenious combination of illusion, theatre, magic and humour, and is typical of the artist, who says, 'I like to reward the onlooker who looks carefully by hiding small treasures in my murals.'

Although trompe l'oeil has been practised since the days of the ancient Greeks, it is not an easy technique to master. It must be life-size if it is to fool the eye and requires infinite skill and a mastery of perspective in order to achieve a realistic three-dimensional effect. Realistic rendering of objects is essential if the onlooker is to be taken in. For that reason, nearly all trompe l'oeil are based on traditional subjects and painted in a technique which goes back to the fifteenth century. There is no such thing as a 'modern' trompe l'oeil, even though the composition can be treated in a contemporary way. Human figures are not successful in trompe l'oeil as they appear frozen and it is also practically impossible to mistake a painted figure for a genuine person.

The artist must tempt you to reach out and pluck a leatherbound book off a shelf, touch a silken Persian carpet lying on the floor or step down an imaginary corridor through seemingly endless doors and out into a fantasy landscape. The trend has been evolving at a steady pace for the past twenty years in both England and America and is more popular today than ever.

The cabinet of curiosities, niches and simulated bookcases laden with dusty tomes, which were popular in seventeenth-century Europe, still inspire muralists. But the sombre skulls, bottled potions and feathered quills such as those in the symbolic Vanitas still-life paintings of the seventeenth-century Dutch artist Cornelius Gijsbrechts have been exchanged for more lighthearted objects today. Tony Raymond has a passion for eighteenth-century paintings, style and *objects d'art*. He gives this enthusiasm full rein in a small shop in the heart of London called Dragons, a treasure trove of unusual paraphernalia (Plate 38). His painted cupboard is full of exquisite eighteenth-century objects and personal mementoes, evoking the treasures attributed to Domenico Remps in his famous *Cabinet of Curiosities*, painted in the late seventeenth century (Opificio delle Pietre Dure, Florence). In the contemporary version, two faience plates delicately patterned with a rose, beetle and tulip stand against a background of Spitalfields silk. A Chinese temple jar and a Chelsea group of shepherd and shepherdess can be seen, resting on a piece of Brussels lace. The early Staffordshire cauliflower coffee pot and pastel-coloured fan are gentle reminders of the finer things in life. Tucked away in the corner is a *Book of Dragons* in honour of the shop. Raymond comments: 'A mural is an individual's decoration. Few people would commission a painting. Instead they would buy one. But having something that is close to the person's ideas and ideals must be part of the equation for their current popularity.'

Simulated shelves can be just as effective as painted cupboards. The contents, along with the titles of the books, provide revealing clues as to the personality of their owner. Besides being easy on the eye, painted shelves full of leatherbound tomes are warm and cosy. For the apartment belonging to his clients Mr and Mrs Samuel P. Reeds, the American decorator and muralist Richard Neas has created an illusionary trompe l'oeil library wall, full of the familiar vocabulary—leatherbound books, personal mementoes and photographs. In front of the books a

38. Tony Raymond. 1985. Flashe, 238 × 143 cm (90 × 54 in). Rosie Fisher

40. Sarah Janson. 1986. Oil on wood, 285 × 222 cm (108 × 84 in). Private collection

39. Garth Benton. Acrylic. Private collection

41. Simon Brady. 1985. Acrylic on board, 100 × 87 cm (38 × 33 in). Private collection

42. Simon Brady. 1986. Acrylic on board, 100 × 87 cm (38 × 33 in). Private collection

43. David Marrian. 1986. Acrylic on board, 127 × 95 cm (48 × 36 in). Mr and Mrs Thomas Hughes-Hallett

painted map marks the route taken by his clients on a memorable trip through Africa and Asia. The two continents are symbolized by a majestically decorated Indian elephant and a solemn rhino painted in the style of Dürer, which had many seventeenth-century imitators.

Dutch artists in the seventeenth century excelled in the visual deception and humour of trompe l'oeil with their skilful interpretation of letter racks and quodlibets (still lifes containing a variety of objects). These compositions were filled with sheets of folded worn paper and engravings together with scissors, seals and other objects tucked behind tape. Moral messages of vanity and melancholy were often incorporated into the compositions to convey human weaknesses. A twisted curl of orange peel symbolized the spiral of life and scissors alluded to life's frailty. The fly was a symbol of mortality, and musical instruments and jewels communicated the pointlessness of possessions and earthly delights. Not surprisingly, with very few exceptions, contemporary muralists eschew lessons in morality.

The trompe l'oeil cupboard or cabinet of curiosities displays objects seemingly placed behind the surface of the wall and away from us. By contrast the three-dimensional effect of letters and documents on a letter rack appear projected forward into our space. In the fifteenth century Carpaccio, a passionate painter of interesting objects, painted one of the earliest trompe l'oeil panels with a length of tape holding a haphazard array of letters and documents on it. On the other side of the wooden panel is depicted a scene entitled *Hunting on the Lagoon*. This early example of a true trompe l'oeil is now owned by the J. Paul Getty Museum in California.

One example of trompe l'oeil which has survived changes in fashion are fireplace panels known as '*les devants de cheminée*', which were used extensively in the eighteenth century. When spring turned to summer and fires were no longer needed, the painted panels fitted neatly into the fireplace, concealing the hearth opening. Apart from seeing them as serving a useful decorative purpose, prospective clients find chimneyboards a small, specific and manageable work of art, rather like a painting, with which to decorate their rooms. They are intensely personal, reflecting the owner's particular life style and often have a mysteriously harmonious quality which expresses the essence of the house and its owner.

Nostalgia is frequently a powerful source of inspiration for these utilitarian works. One successful example can be seen in an old house in Belgium, painted by the young English muralist Simon Brady (Plate 41). The greatest influence in his work has been his passion for antiquities. This was fired by working in the sculpture and metalwork department at Sotheby's for five years where he greatly admired the Renaissance bronzes. In the architectural theme for his fake mantelpiece, he uses eighteenth-century props in a distinctly twentieth-century fashion. Behind the creamy ivory-covered scagliola columns topped with gilt metal, lies a darkened background of black streaked marble and red porphyry topped by what he describes as a 'bit of Empire nonsense'. Scagliola is an imitation marble so there is, in effect, a double trompe l'oeil—a fake within a fake. The graceful Louis XV terracotta urn with swans is flanked by two porcelain urns with gilt mounts. On the polished marble floor lies a cartellino, painted as part of trompe l'oeil since the fifteenth century, and bearing Simon Brady's signature.

Apart from evoking the mysterious background corners of a real fireplace, chimneyboards need relatively strong foreground lighting to project the objects into the spectator's space. The English painter David Marrian has depicted a hearth with exposed bricks serving as a darkened background, for his clients Jules and Thomas Hughes-Hallett (Plate 43). Against this hangs a blackened frying pan and bunches of lavender taken from their garden. The gentle light on the curves of the Ming vase and porcelain bowl, together with the rounded shadow, softens the firm rectangular space of the fireplace. A couple of bottles of Bordeaux are waiting to be opened, tantalizingly, and two books remind the viewer that the pleasures of this house are not only to do with drinking and eating.

44. Richard Shirley Smith. 1980. Oil. Private collection

Larger than a trompe l'oeil chimneyboard, but just as effective, screens were first used over two thousand years ago. Painted screens have only entered our homes since the end of the nineteenth century. Cezanne, Bonnard and Duncan Grant were among the artists who tried their hand at decorating these versatile pieces of furniture. Many twentieth-century screens are regarded as an art form in their own right. Apart from dividing off a room, hiding an unattractive but essential piece of furniture or simply making an area more intimate, a beautifully painted screen can enhance the look of a room in much the same way as a painting.

Ian Cairnie, a youthful and energetic English decorative artist who teaches trompe l'oeil painting at the Inchbald School of Design in London, has achieved this with a five-panelled screen painted for a house in Spain (Plate 45). His intention was to evoke the open spaces of southern Spain with its common bird, the hoopoe, standing proudly beneath a potted orange tree bursting with ripened fruit. The fulness of the rounded tree is in sharp contrast to the slim datura plant with its delicate white flowers reaching to the top of the screen. Cairnie has cleverly managed to give an impression of a balcony by depicting the bottom third of the screen as a ledge. The small perfect shells, china and terracotta pots as well as the hoopoe on the painted false ledge project forward into our space. This traditional trompe l'oeil device creates a feeling of lightness and harmony as the viewer gazes out over the romantic landscape.

Ian Cairnie is a versatile and exceptionally talented muralist who can tackle any style of mural, from painting tight nineteenth-century style scenes to loose adaptions based on Matisse cutouts. He feels that the ideas and process of his work 'should be more important than the execution, although of course I want everything to look ravishing. I work quickly and feel there is some kind of pride in so doing, although it's odd that in a world where there are so many variables it should come down to how fast you can do it.' He sees himself as essentially a decorative artist. Cairnie turned to painting as an escape into fantasy from loneliness, the result of being an only child living above his parents' grocery shop.

Small and intimate rooms have always been a favoured subject for painters; the challenge to expand the space successfully is all the greater. One of the earliest pictorial renderings of this theme was the scholar's cell, with its incentive to meditate and study, which was so frequently portrayed from the fifteenth century onwards. Dürer's engraving of *St Jerome in his Study* perfectly depicts this intimate world of books and solitude.

A particularly successful example of the skilful expansion of limited space can be seen in Roy Alderson's house. On opening the door of a small cupboard which is now the guest room, the visitor comes across a detailed replica of Queen Adelaide's railway coach. Built in 1842, it was one of the first sleeping coaches to be made (Plate 47). As the story goes, the unfortunate Queen's feet stuck out over the end of her bed, something that the artist's lucky guests no longer have to endure. Only the blue velvet-covered bed, the television and its curtains, as well as the carriage light, are real. The rest is illusion. The dusty blue room is a cosy retreat from reality for the occupier. The imagined rhythm of the wheels, pulling him through the Scottish countryside, lulls him to sleep.

Roy Alderson, like a number of artists, gets ideas and inspiration for his murals from books on old wallpapers. Those known as Papiers Peints were expensive and beautifully produced wallpapers made in early nineteenth-century Europe. Jean Zuber, the French wallpaper manufacturer, was famous for producing 'Panoramiques', scenic wallpaper which unfolded into a continuous scene around the walls of a room. This eliminated the messy procedure of pasting up separate sheets on the wall. The romantic themes included exotic flora and fauna, palm trees and natives in rich vibrant colours. The designs contained an abundance of sky and ground at the top and bottom of the paper which was snipped to fit the height of the room.

Sarah Janson, one of England's few successful and talented women muralists, painted simulated folds of drapes along the walls of a small bathroom in her house (Plate 53). The idea for the mural was inspired by a Papier

45. Ian Cairnie. 1986. Oil on wood, 190 × 238 cm (72 × 90 in). Mr and Mrs David Bulmer

Peint wallpaper printed by Joseph Dufour in 1815. The drapes are held together with soft gold tassels which accentuate the tautness of caught fabric and the tactile reality of material. The elegant classical feel of the folds with their intricate lighting, is softened by the creamy yellow background of the bathroom walls with their handpainted laurel motif peeking out from under the drapes.

Simulated materials are most often used on walls, but they can be used just as effectively on the floor. The richly detailed patterns and sensual texture of Persian carpets have been a distinctive addition woven into the paintings of classical times. A carpet is seen hanging over a balustrade in Carlo Crivelli's *Annunciation* (c.1486), now in the National Gallery, London. In the paintings of Hans Holbein (1497–1543), such as his portrait of Thomas Cromwell in the Frick Collection, New York, his exquisite renditions of oriental rugs on dining tables eventually caused them to become known as 'Holbein carpets'.

Lucretia Moroni, a protegée of the great Italian architect and designer Lorenzo Mongiardino, has painted the parquet floors of Stavros Niarchos' large Manhattan living room to resemble a series of seventeenth-century Persian carpets (Plate 48). Moroni, who now lives in New York, enjoys painting the complexities of textiles more than any other trompe l'oeil object and has designed a distinctive background colour for each of the three separate

46. Alan Dodd. 1977. Oil with sand, 158 × 190 cm (60 × 72 in). (Cartouche surrounding painting by Bison (c.1780) and to complement five panels by Domenico Tiepolo.) Private collection

47. Roy Alderson. 1964. Oil, 507 × 253 cm (192 × 96 in). Artist's collection

rugs—red, blue and greeny-blue. Parts of each rug were silkscreened directly onto the floor. Decorations for the intricate borders and centres were applied with the use of handcut stencils. Over twenty different colours and patterns were used in each rug. The artist achieved the unusually soft three-dimensional effect by painting different geometric and floral patterns over a pointillist background. (Pointillism was the Impressionist technique of covering the canvas with dots of colour which blend together, producing an overall cohesion.) Moroni is a perfectionist. She mixes each colour herself from pure water-based pigments imported from Italy to achieve exactly the right shade. Old Persian rugs were made with pure pigments and sometimes washed in salt water and dried in the sun to get a lighter colour, all of which was carefully observed by the artist before embarking on this huge project. The beautiful floorpaintings, which look totally convincing as precious carpets, are sealed with a mixture of high gloss and satin varnish to imitate the shine on antique silk rugs.

Hunting trophies in which dead animals and birds are surrounded with all the paraphernalia of the hunter, are another favourite trompe l'oeil subject. These paintings often decorated the walls of palaces and middle-class interiors from the sixteenth century onwards; royalty commissioned paintings of trophies following their traditional deer hunts. The nineteenth-century American artists William Michael Harnett, John Frederick Peto and John Haberle are the inspiration behind many of the paintings of hunting trophies executed in America and England. Their work was intensely American and based on ordinary domestic paraphernalia: dead game and guns, hunting objects and flasks, hats and horns, all nailed to a wooden door or panel. These hunting trophies adorned numerous hunting rooms throughout America and were an important part of the lives of the pioneers. It was natural to have them painted for posterity.

The English artist Jonathan Brunskill, whose strength lies in including inanimate objects within an architectural framework, has painted a 'hunting trophy' trompe l'oeil in grisaille in the London dining room of master chef Anton Mossiman (Plate 50). Brunskill's composition, based on the taking and recycling of life, also incorporates the idea of a larder together with a cabinet of curiosities. The curtain was added to create more depth and in allusion to the seventeenth century, when curtains were placed over cupboards instead of doors. Curtains are an ancient trompe l'oeil device. In around 400 BC the Greek painter Zeuxis was fooled by his great rival and contemporary, Parrhasius. Demanding that the drapery covering a painting of Parrhasius be pulled aside, Zeuxis was mortified to find the curtain itself was painted.

Musical instruments, false niches and shelves laden with domestic objects also play an important part in the trompe l'oeil artist's repertoire. They can be used in the smallest spaces. The delicacy of the violin, together with the sensuous curve of its base and the subtle patina of varnished wood has always attracted artists. As a small and relatively shallow object, it is the perfect musical instrument for a trompe l'oeil panel. Jonathan Brunskill has placed one against a painted pine cupboard door and held it in place by a soft silk bow (Plate 52). A sheet of Brahms' music is tucked behind the instrument and the cast shadow brings the simple lines of the violin out in sharp relief—reminiscent of the famous illusionary example in the music room at Chatsworth House, home of the duke and duchess of Devonshire, which is attributed to Jan van der Vaart (1647–1721).

Simulated niches have found their way into this art form since the sixteenth century when they first became an important aspect of decoration in European palaces and churches. Then they held painted statues of saints in imitation marble (grisaille) which were apparently set back into the niches. Instead of niches holding marble statues of saints, the ubiquitous plant is the current fashion. In the foyer of an international company outside London, Lincoln Seligman has created visual interest with two simulated niches (Plate 51). Instead of including luscious green tropical specimens, he has painted two plants in grisaille, in the same pale granite material as the walls of the building. Seligman says that if murals are not visually complicated, people frequently

49. Christian Thee. 1977. Acrylic on wood, 222 × 158 cm (84 × 60 in). Artist's collection

48. (*previous page*) Lucretia Moroni. 1984. Water-based pigments. Stavros Niarchos

50. Jonathan Brunskill. 1985. Acrylic, 190 × 190 cm (72 × 72 in) or 285 × 79 cm (108 × 30 in).
Mr and Mrs Anton Mossiman

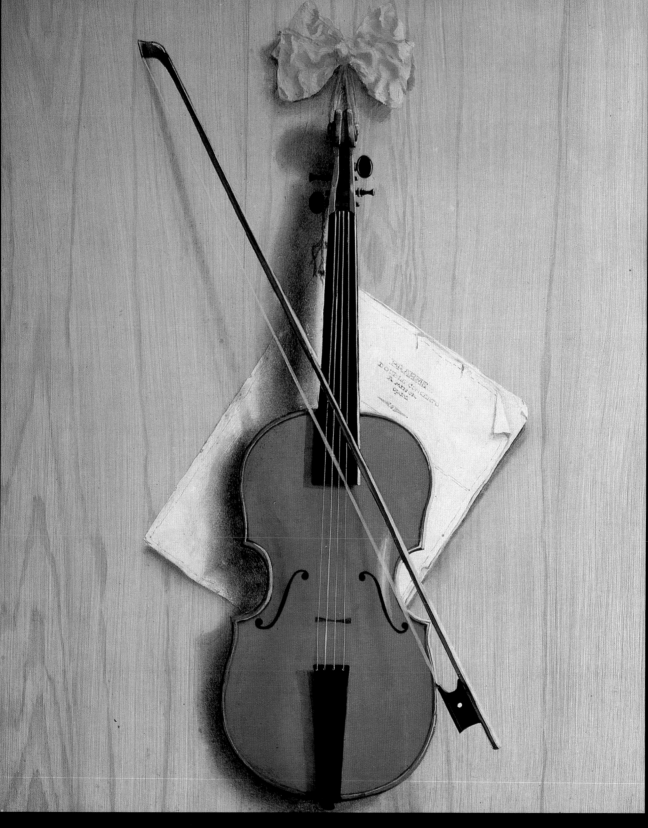

52. Jonathan Brunskill. 1984. Oil on wood. 74 × 48 cm (28 × 18 in). Artist's collection

think that not much intellectual effort has gone into them.

Glass cases full of insects, stuffed birds or rare butterflies emerge as trompe l'oeil subjects whenever the genre attains renewed popularity. 'The case of the broken butterflies' could well be the title of a modern whodunit. In fact, this particular trompe l'oeil was the brainchild of American painter Lincoln Taber, who lives in England and whose inspiration was a visit by his local vicar. A little merry, the parson fell back onto a case of rare butterflies, smashed the glass and destroyed a couple of the exotic creatures inside. Taber decided to immortalize them in all their damaged beauty, with the broken glass, which is still there today (Plate 57). The painting was exhibited at the Royal Academy's summer exhibition in 1979 and caused unease in some spectators with the dead fly which is stuck to the bottom of the case with a large pearl-headed pin. But after all the butterflies are pinned to the panel, so why not a fly, the symbol of mortality in classical times?

Lincoln Taber, a hospitable man given to laughter, is a well-known portrait painter, his most famous painting being a portrait of Princess Anne. He lived in Florence and for seven out of his ten years there he studied under the renowned Italian painter, Pietro Annigoni. Along with other artists, he made a copy of the Sistine chapel in St Peter's Basilica in Rome for the film *The Agony and the Ecstasy* on the life of Michelangelo.

One of the most difficult tricks to pull off in trompe l'oeil is the three-dimensional illusion which is to be viewed from every angle, such as a large simulated mantelpiece. Ian Cairnie achieves this with considerable skill at Brilley Court, home of Rosanna and David Bulmer, where he has painted a mantelpiece with an acanthus design and egg and dart ends (Plate 56). The eye level is placed in the middle of the lower mantel so that the illusion is realistically appreciated from a seated, as well as a standing position. The whole image gives an imposing impression of heightened grandeur. The illusionary mantel is filled with 'dramatis personae', including personal books and photos of the country house, vases of freshly picked roses, black tulips and lilies from the garden and an oil painting of ducks borrowed from an Ackermann's catalogue. The mural is painted in oil, which Cairnie prefers for its richness as he feels it has more life in it and is easier to glaze with.

Trompe l'oeil paintings, whether a cartouche framing an Old Master painting or a black and red Dutch floor with its teasing display of cards and books of poetry, create the impression of total realism. They may be a nostalgic reminder of the past or an unattainable dream world but the fascination of humour and visual deception is irresistible for many of us.

53. Sarah Janson. 1986. Water-based paint, 317 × 253 cm (120 × 96 in). Artist's collection

54. Carlos Marchiori. *Pompeiiana*. Acrylic on wood. 253 × 190 cm (96 × 72 in). Private collection

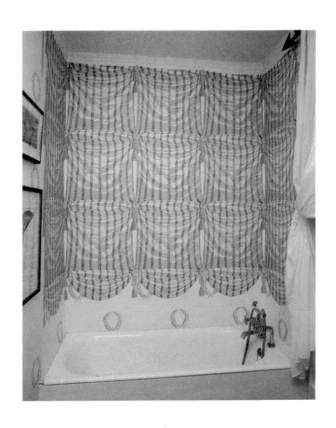

56. Ian Cairnie. 1983. Oil, 190 × 127 cm (72 × 48 in).
Mr and Mrs David Bulmer

55. Ian Cairnie. 1983. Oil, 190 × 127 cm (72 × 48 in) (*detail of Plate 56*). Mr and Mrs David Bulmer

57. Lincoln Taber. 1975. Oil, 63 × 63 cm (24 × 24 in). Lord Tanlaw

58. Graham Rust. 1985. Flashe, 539 × 253 cm (204 × 96 in). Private collection

59. (*overleaf*) Lincoln Seligman. 1985. Acrylic, 792 × 570 cm (300 × 216 in). BBDO Advertising Agency, London

60. (*overleaf*) Douglas Riseborough. Acrylic, 15·84 × 3·17 m (50 × 10 ft). U.C.L.A., Los Angeles, California

CORPORATE AND COMMERCIAL MURALS

The popularity of exterior public art—pop art, graffiti and the revolt against the urban jungle—reached its zenith in the last decade. The obvious next step was for the mural to retreat indoors, become more personal and embellish our homes. More recently, led predictably by the Americans, the mural has invaded the corporate sanctuary. Companies in the United States are the modern Medici and they are more open to the bizarre and progressive in murals.

The rising enthusiasm in architectural circles for decorative treatments of corporate buildings, restaurants, churches and universities, is largely due to the Post-Modern reaction against the austere Bauhaus International Style of architecture. Famous as an avant-garde institution, the Bauhaus was founded in Germany by the modernist architect Walter Gropius immediately after his country's defeat in World War I. A collaboration of art, sculpture and architecture, its drastically simplified functional style was to have an immense impact on design during the following decades. Nazi Germany, intent on persecuting modernism, forced its closure in 1933, with the result that many of its architects, designers and artists—such as Wassily Kandinsky, Max Beckmann, Paul Klee and Hans Hofmann—fled to the relative freedom of America and the rest of Europe, particularly France. Here they helped to influence and shape the future art of these countries.

Under America's tax incentives, large corporations can commission murals and artwork at virtually no real cost. American companies are also more aware of the corporate image than their British counterparts, who deem culture and computers odd bedfellows and are wary of large visual statements adorning their offices. As James Hurford, an architect with Powell Moya and Partners, who designed the imposing Queen Elizabeth II Conference Centre opposite Westminster Abbey, says: 'Large corporations are not particularly interested in art and it will always be a minority of architects who want art in buildings, concerned as they are that the art might overshadow the architecture. This is especially so considering we have only just emerged from the bleak mid-winter of modernism.' A British Government circular put out in 1985 states that any public building wishing to spend more than the princely sum of £500 on art must receive specific ministerial permission. The Conference Centre now owns and borrows more paintings, sculptures and wallhangings than any other government building in Britain.

Corporations in England are understandably concerned about the cost of commissioning works of art, since these do not enjoy tax concessions; to say nothing of the potential for office disruption while a mural is being painted and the time-consuming business of finding the right artist. A modest tax concession, along American lines, for British companies interested in commissioning works of art would give a huge boost to the United Kingdom art scene, especially murals.

One main difference between the two countries is the state funding of the creative arts. In America, buildings locally funded by state or city must allocate one per cent of the development cost to art. If the artwork is not to be used directly in the proposed building, then the one per cent must be distributed to the public area, through the auspices of the city.

In England, on the other hand, while the performing arts receive some financial help, government incentives offered to the visual arts are far less benevolent. In 1987 the Arts Council of Great Britain gave £138 million to the performing arts, compared with £107 million to the visual arts, to cover museums, galleries and libraries. Also the British business community has proved a less than reliable patron in commissioning large works of art, which up until now have mainly been funded by the public purse.

Many big American corporations have devoted large amounts of money to the sponsorship of art, but few on the scale of the Equitable Life Assurance Society of America which has spent over $7 million on commissioning or acquiring art in the last few years. Apart from housing a small branch of the Whitney Museum, a number of huge works of art can be seen in its East Tower in Manhattan.

An enormous billboard-like Lichtenstein mural dominates the foyer, Thomas Hart Benton's 1931 *America Today* lines one wall, and Sandro Chia's powerful multicoloured mural can be found in the Palio Restaurant. Other large companies which have commissioned murals and works of art include Metropolitan Life Assurance, IBM, Philip Morris, Coca-Cola and the Security Pacific Bank in Los Angeles.

Many of the American artists mentioned in these chapters are involved in art for offices as well as other commercial enterprises. In England they are thinner on the ground. A notable exception is the enterprising Lincoln Seligman. An Oxford scholar and former barrister, he gave up law ten years ago to paint full time. He was determined to elicit corporate patronage as he found the restrictions imposed on his output in private homes too confining. Being a humorous man, he thinks corporate murals should be both thought-provoking and slightly tongue-in-cheek interpretations of the company involved.

Seligman is among the highest paid muralists in England. His mural for the world's sixth largest advertising agency, BBDO International, is a good example of his wit, with its send-up of the hype in advertising. A classical Adam room is shattered by the sacred icons of the advertising world bursting through the walls and floating in space—the frantic telephone, the ubiquitous earphones and cassettes, brains and chips for the executive too busy to stop for lunch. The brains were the artist's indulgent fantasy of advertising being the corporate equivalent of fast food. 'I imagine that the brain of the average advertising man would be completely indigestible,' says Seligman. Influenced by Magritte, Seligman enjoys taking things out of their plane in his paintings, with the effect of jarring the viewer and making him uncomfortable (Plate 59).

For a corporation to commission a mural requires more courage and imagination than money. BBDO, something of a trail-blazer among British companies, asked Seligman to produce another mural. *2085 Man for Unleaded Fuel* (Plate 61) depicts a transparent man who grew up in the 1960s and retained much of the conflicting guilt connected with that era. He joins in protest marches and worries about the Third World and acid rain while

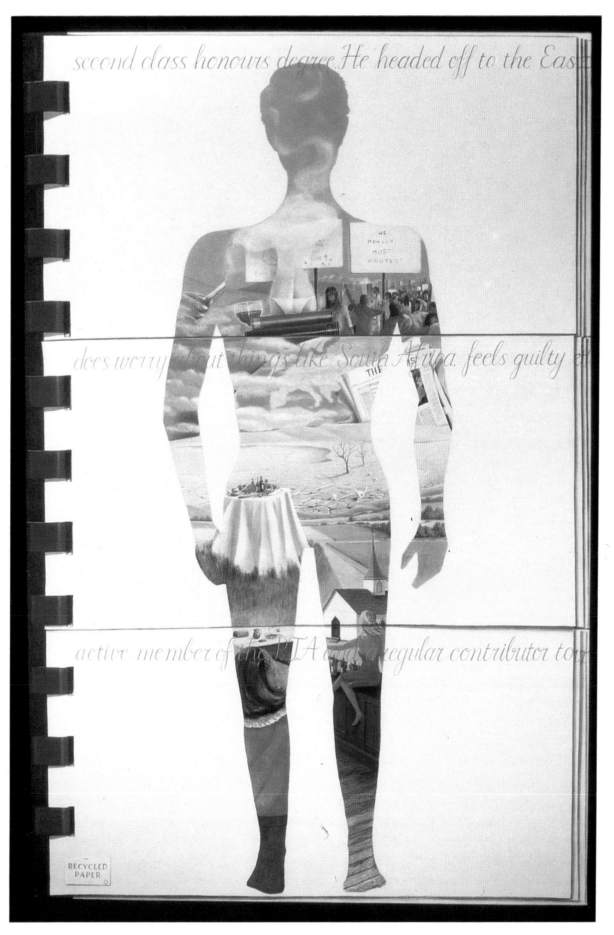

61. Lincoln Seligman. *2085 Man for Unleaded Fuel*. 1986. Acrylic on canvas, 190 × 127 cm (72 × 48 in). BBDO Advertising Agency for Kuwait Petroleum Inc., London

eating expensive lunches and dreaming about nubile women. He would use unleaded petrol and never buy Cape fruit but that is about as far as his involvement leads him.

The American art world is unique in that it harbours muralists who design murals for gigantic buildings which are then carried out by other painters. The most prolific is Richard Haas, whose outdoor architectural representation and rendered façades have become famous landmarks of downtown Manhattan, and were the first of their kind. Haas' monumental outdoor achievements are among the most original contemporary concepts in murals. Fascinated by historical styles of architecture and despairing of the modern (he has said, 'Cities in America don't work—they are just stretched-out pockets of activity'), Haas determined to change the harsh urban environment through the use of murals, preferring to depict the earlier sympathetic and delicate skyscrapers of the 1920s.

He often works in close association with architects from the beginning of a project, recently with the firm Voorsanger and Mills on the New York University Midtown Center for which he designed different views of Manhattan. He no longer paints any of the commissions himself, preferring to delegate the huge task to other painters. The difficulty of this is in knowing how to relinquish touch control on almost every level and still maintain the huge murals as his own work. He compares the problem to those of the Renaissance artists, whom he likens to 'the General Motors of their time', employing and overseeing the numerous painters who worked for them. Haas refers to his murals as 'site specific' and 'architecturally related art', and since he designs huge projects, he tends to think more on a corporate level than an individual one.

Haas' murals painted for interiors tend to be more elaborately detailed. His *Installation of a Room* (Plate 62) was one of four schematic rooms designed for an exhibition which travelled to two American art galleries and then to the University of Tennessee. The rooms were representative of an era, in this case the 1920s and 1930s, and music was composed for each room, from Balinese chimes to tones from Mahler, stressing the interrelationship between art, architecture and music.

On the West Coast, Haas' colleague Terry Schoonhaven paints murals dictated by different senses and values. The bright light and wide open spaces provide a sense of freedom for muralists not found in eastern cities, and the transparency of Los Angeles, with its film industry and inherent sense of illusion, is well suited to Schoonhaven's ironic environmental wallpaintings. As the Chicago-born artist says, 'It doesn't seem illogical to drop images in this city.' Architecture in Los Angeles is not very precious (buildings get torn down all the time) and the constant creation of new walls provides enormous scope for the wilder shores of the muralists' imagination. This concept is entirely alien to Europeans, who expect their buildings and their murals to last.

A loner and permanent do-it-yourself addict when it comes to painting his own murals, Schoonhaven is firmly rooted in California. He explains, 'Since this city is responsible for my painting murals at all, Los Angeles is naturally my inspiration. I have no other dreams or illusions about painting. This is it.' He, Kent Twitchell and a number of other artists are responsible for the massive outdoor murals along one of Los Angeles' main freeways which were commissioned for the 1984 Olympics.

Schoonhaven is best known for portraying huge empty spaces. His interest lies in taking an interior space and emptying it, giving the area a strange, deserted effect. He feels the inclusion of people establishes a barrier between the viewer and the work, losing a certain responsiveness to the empty stage quality. Captivated by the Indian dwellings of Mesa Verde in Colorado, Schoonhaven longed to place them in a mural. When he was commissioned to do a large mural in the Bank of Denver, it seemed natural to transfer his fascination onto the wall, both places being in Colorado. Ambiguous relationships occur in the mural in terms of materials and structure. The stone dwellings of the original were substituted with the city of Denver and the artist combined the

62. Richard Haas. *Installation of a Room*. 1982. Acrylic, 380 × 507 cm (144 × 192 in). Artist's collection

63. Hank Prussing. 1975–78.
Acrylic. Lafayette Avenue
Presbyterian Church,
Brooklyn, New York

feel of the two by an elaborate process of creating the city buildings to appear as if they were mockups of buildings to look like stone and then coloured to resemble cliff dwellings (Plate 64).

Churches and universities, with their relevant links to the surrounding community, could again become a focal point for muralists' work. Although it is rare these days for a church to commission wallpaintings, mural painting in medieval England was the most practised of all the arts and decorated many of the largest churches and palaces in the country. These delicate ornamentations were destroyed by the Reformers who blindly removed all painted decorations from abbeys and churches. Also, there have been other periods of artistic blight, especially after the separation of the artist from his traditional patron, the Church, in the wake of the Baroque period. Many churches now, especially in Britain, need every penny they have to repair the fabric of the building and cannot afford to commission wallpaintings. But very slowly and with no fanfare, ideas for beautifying a few church interiors are changing, perhaps as one way of drawing the faithful back into the fold. Following the example of the sumptuously decorated Renaissance churches, Lambeth Palace, home of the archbishops of Canterbury since the late twelfth century, has commissioned a vast mural for the chapel's ceiling, to be done by English artist Leonard Rosoman, thus indicating a long-overdue reunion between Church and artist. One possible solution for the future would be for private individuals to commission more work in churches.

Church decoration in America is attuned to the surrounding community. The upper balcony of Lafayette Avenue Presbyterian church, a nineteenth-century church in Brooklyn, New York, bristles with the activity of its painted community acting out their everyday affairs (Plate 63). The artist, Hank Prussing, who was first called in as an architect to renovate the church, became fascinated by the similarities in the symbolism of the church's magnificent Tiffany-era art-glass windows and the realities of the neighbourhood street life beyond the church's walls. As he explained, 'I roamed the streets, snapping hundreds of candid photos of people strolling, running, playing, talking and sitting. When I examined the images—random non-events of everyday existence—they exhibited the same underlying traits of human nature that shone through the church's windows.' The result, *Clouds of Witness*, is a portrait of a richly diverse neighbourhood, each section of the wall exploring a different aspect of human nature.

This enthusiasm has spilled over into California's halls of learning. Two universities in Los Angeles have commissioned murals by two of the state's most prolific artists. At Loyola Law School, Kent Twitchell collaborated with well-known Los Angeles artist Jim Morphesis in portraying *The Fall of Icarus* in a 22-foot mural (Plate 65). The myth, which has come to symbolize human striving for god-like ideals and justice with the inevitable human failure and renewed effort, was painted in numerous vibrant colours and shapes to build up form over many layers of gesso, giving the mural a certain translucent quality. The wall and its huge figure of Icarus falling from the sky with one of his wings melting is painted in an elaborate pattern, almost as if modelled on 'painting-by-numbers'. The deep reds fade into golds and white, creating a powerful effect.

Another artist whose work has a strong moral content—justice and racial harmony—is Douglas Riseborough. The quiet atmosphere of the U.C.L.A. law library is disrupted by a massive figurative portrayal of the social problems found in America (Plate 60). The first segment of the 50-foot mural, entitled *The Journey*, deals with the problem of racism. It is dominated by the huge face of a suffering black man, surrounded by angry and anguished figures striving to break free from prejudice. The centre panel, *Regeneration*, conveys the need for each emerging generation to maintain the spirit of justice, while the third panel highlights the social unrest that follows the unfulfilled expectations of the young.

A self-trained artist, Riseborough approaches painting as an exercise in draughtsmanship with colour so that the painting will hold the vitality of a drawing. In all of his works, which are painted on vast canvases, the

64. Terry Schoonhaven. *Cliff Palace*. 1983. Acrylic on linen, 444 × 697 cm (168 × 264 in). United Bank of Denver, Denver, Colorado

66. Garth Benton. 1972. Acrylic on canvas. J. Paul Getty Museum, Malibu, California

65. Kent Twitchell and Jim Morphesis. 1984–85. Marcus mural paint, 665 × 665 cm (252 × 252 in).
Loyola University, Los Angeles, California

67. Robin Archer and Emma
    Temple. 1986. Oil (*detail*).
    J. Lyons Wimbledon
    Pavilion

human form dominates, with the detail and the background playing a secondary role. Riseborough's main inspiration comes from the great figurative painters, Michelangelo, Goya, Veronese, El Greco and Velasquez, and the 'fire and ice of the Mexican muralists' figurative work'.

Murals which appeal to our social conscience are worlds apart from commercial enterprises which are trying to sell a particular commodity. The large mural which London-based commercial artist Carmel Said produced for Laura Ashley's company is reminiscent of paintings of house interiors by the Dutch artist Vermeer in the seventeenth century (Plate 68). The soft colouring of the interior is a harmonious backdrop for the perfectly rendered trompe l'oeil leather chest on the floor in the front of the picture, compelling the viewer to define where the mural ends and the real floor begins.

Architects designing public buildings have tended to shy away from frescoes and murals because of a lack of durability. The laborious and time-consuming art of painting fresco onto the plaster is no longer practical for the mural painter; moreover the plaster is vulnerable to cracking in this sonic age. But the modern mediums of acrylic, indelible gouache (Flashe) and outdoor emulsions such as Keim are resistant to water and can withstand hazards like pollution, making murals a far less vulnerable and delicate art form than they once were.

Large amounts of money are involved in the commissioning of murals in America and since the occupancy of buildings is relatively short, owing to the transitory nature of both owner and building, most murals are painted on canvas which is either stretched onto the wall or placed within panels, and then removed along with the potted plants to the next place of residence.

The idea of contract painting—carrying out the designs of others—is unknown in England. In America, however, in a colourful and hectic studio behind an old store front in lower Manhattan a group of highly involved artists have formed a remarkable cooperative. Founded by Jeff Greene, an unusually philanthropic and energetic man, Evergreene Studios is based on the proprietor's preference for emphasizing the collaborative nature of mural painting rather than individual expression. 'After all,' he says, 'the whole idea of working totally alone is only a couple of hundred years old and individual artists can't paint on the same scale we can.' Greene designs much of the work produced by his studio, and is committed to a high degree of craftsmanship from his artists in the finished work.

Disillusioned with the world of fine art, Greene set out to establish the contemporary equivalent of a William Morris studio. Each member of his studio has his own area of expertise—drafting, colour, glazing, marbling—while Greene does much of the figurative work for the murals. As Greene says, 'We must learn and be guided by artists who, in the past were so eloquent in this visual language, but we must also form our own new language and expression. The tradition of superb craftsmanship has been lost here, but in England they really care about it being done well.' He is totally at ease in executing many of the designs of other artists such as Richard Haas' design for the lobby of the Chestnut Place apartments in Chicago (Plate 69). It is painted in the style of the church of San Miniato al Monte in Florence, a combination of trompe l'oeil pillars and balustrades surrounded by a wealth of delicately patterned *faux marbre* covering the floor, walls and ceiling.

Most of the best muralists in America work on the East and West Coasts. Lately Texas, with its abundant wealth and upward mobility, is proving a profitable hunting ground for muralists. Local corporations, keen to polish their cultured image, are embellishing their offices with works of art. Delmas Howe, an easel painter and muralist based in Truth or Consequences, New Mexico, travels all over America on commission. For a speech and hearing centre in Amarillo, Texas, with the logo of a shell, Howe painted numerous large-scale species floating through an otherwise bland institution (Plate 70). As the facility is used by many children who need entertaining, he joined the images with long painted streamers or 'waves', enabling the shells to flow through the

68. Carmel Said. 1985. Emulsion, 317 × 380 cm (120 × 144 in). Laura Ashley

69. Evergreene Studios (Richard Haas design). 1982. *Faux marbre*. Chestnut Street Lobby, Chicago, Illinois

70. Delmas Howe. Vinyl ink on vinyl walls. Amarillo Speech and Hearing Centre, Amarillo Texas

71. Delmas Howe. Oil on canvas, 792 × 412 cm (300 × 156 in). Texas and Southwestern Cattleraisers' Association, Fort Worth, Texas

72. Laura Gerahty. 1983. Encaustic paint, 634 cm (240 in) diameter. Chenil Gallery, London

73. (*overleaf*)Ted Seth Jacobs. 1979. Acrylic. Regency Plaza Hotel, New York

building and help reduce the huge emptiness of the space. He also completed a 25-foot cowboy mural for the Cattleraisers' Foundation in Fort Worth, Texas. Apart from filling a cavernous space, the subject matter had to be one dear to the cattleraisers' hearts. The result is a realistic, although romantic, depiction of cowboy life in the 'Big Sky' country (Plate 71).

Today, antique and art galleries are considered aesthetic spaces suitable for showing off murals. The Chenill Gallery on the King's Road, London, now full of antiques, was originally an art gallery and the brainchild of the painter, Augustus John. Used as a pioneering centre for the arts, it had the first one-man shows of Augustus John, Eric Gill, David Bomberg and Mark Gertler. Inspired by the figures around Greek vases, artist Laura Gerahty, a young Irish painter who was trained at the Ruskin and learned fresco in Italy, painted the dome of the gallery as a continually moving picture of the people involved in its beginning in 1920. Among the floating figures are the Sitwells, who delighted in putting on performances of *Façade* in the gallery, and Gwen John, sister of Augustus, with her beloved cat, Tiger (Plate 72).

The English artist Althea Wilson uses the downstairs of her London house as an art gallery. It is a continuation of the Elizabethan theme of the house, which is full of heavy Tudor carved oak furniture set against wallpaintings based on Italian Renaissance and English seventeenth-century design. An African jungle mural inspired by a childhood upbringing in Nigeria stretches along one wall of the gallery (Plate 74). One of the artist's own jungle paintings hangs over the mantelpiece. The yellow-bellied toucans lend an extra touch of colour to complement the mural with its plethora of green plants and scarlet African flame tree flowers.

Murals in hotels and restaurants, unfortunately, have a higher mortality rate than most others and many artists have no faith in their work there being preserved for more than a few years. The entrance to the elegant dining room of the Regency Hotel in New York is brought alive by a wonderfully executed mural by New York artist Ted Seth Jacobs, a respected teacher of drawing and painting at the New York Academy of Art. Painted in grisaille against a background of imitation streaked blue marble, a refined and realistic statue with a cornucopia of fruit overflowing at her feet, welcomes diners to the restaurant (Plate 73). Covering the walls inside the restaurant are pale renditions of half-real, half-fantasy French châteaux with a faded tapestry-like quality, which are placed inside elaborate panels (Plate 76).

Restaurants and hotels may be greedy for short-lived murals to attract potential clients, but museums with their philanthropic interest in longevity are other institutions which are also interested in the revival of this art form. Sir Roy Strong, when director of the Victoria and Albert Museum in London, commissioned two artists, Alan Dodd and Jonathan Brunskill, to transform a gloomy director's dining room into an imposing expanse dotted with architectural capricci (Plate 75). Brunskill painted massive trompe l'oeil stone walls in a warm shade of brown and included a fake door in the corner to balance the real one at the opposite end of the room. Alan Dodd's five mural panels incorporate the five styles of European decoration in quiet colours. He included the diminutive figure of Sir Roy peering over the balustrade in a mischievous panel celebrating English Palladianism.

Dodd, a former art teacher and student of the Royal Academy of Art, painted each mural as it would have been in the period it was representing. His Renaissance mural is an amalgam of bits of a wooden screen transmuted into a stone arch, complete with a winking bust to lighten up the heavy subject matter. Through it is glimpsed a room based on the Great Chamber at Hardwick Hall in Derbyshire, with a Jacobean table laden with silver and silvergilt, all of which are in the museum's collection. The mural is bathed in a strange light, giving off a melancholic atmosphere. Dodd feels strongly that the shadows in his paintings must be coloured and not just monochrome, taking their cue from the strongest colour available in the room. The screen in the room comes from Oxford University and is part of the capriccio element, since upper chambers do not usually have screens in

75. Alan Dodd and Jonathan Brunskill. 1986. Oil on canvas, five 253 × 127 cm (96 × 48 in) panels. Victoria and Albert Museum, London

76. Ted Seth Jacobs. 1979. Acrylic. Regency Plaza Hotel, New York

74. (*previous page*) Althea Wilson. 1987. Acrylic, 253 × 380cm (96 × 144in). Althea Wilson Gallery, Chelsea, London

77. Leonard Rosoman. *A Lovely View of Regent's Park*. 1970. Acrylic on wood panels, 3·17 × 10·45 m (120 × 396 in). London School of Business Studies, London

them. The artist's recipe was to create something on the surface of the wall through which another illusion is glimpsed.

'I'm always trying to avoid being called a pasticheur, when painting murals—it's a continuing tradition,' exclaims Dodd, who has very little interest in obtaining commissions from large corporations, 'Small is beautiful as far as I am concerned.' He is also a surrealist and miniature still-life painter. He sees mural painting as an extension of architecture and thinks the most important technique in mural painting is to get the tone right for the atmosphere of the room. Also, that muralists should never be completely fixed by perspective: 'After all, painting tricks are at your service to try and make your statement.' A painter who started art school at the age of fifteen, in the days when one could start young, he recalls that among his most poignant moments as an adolescent was drawing the celebrated English wit, Quentin Crisp, almost the first model he ever drew. An articulate man, with the air of a professor, Dodd bemoans today's art school ideas. 'What I would prefer to teach about mural painting would be regarded as reactionary rubbish. They teach environmental design really,' he says.

In corporate murals with a controversial theme, problems can arise when a capitalist patron employs a left-wing artist. In 1933 Nelson Rockefeller commissioned Diego Rivera to paint a mural in the new RCA Building in New York's Rockefeller Center, on the theme of man's choice for the future. Belatedly realizing the irony of a Communist painter's painting left-wing subjects on a Rockefeller wall, complete with a face of Lenin and the colour red, Rockefeller fired Rivera after paying his full fee. The controversy inspired E.B. White's acerbic ballad 'I Paint What I See'.

'What do you paint, when you paint on a wall?'
　　Said John D.'s grandson Nelson.
　　'Do you paint just anything there at all?
　　Will there be any doves, or a tree in fall?
　　Or a hunting scene, like an English hall?'

'I paint what I see', said Rivera.

'What are the colours you use when you paint?'
　　Said John D.'s grandson Nelson.
　　'Do you use any red in the beard of a saint?
　　If you do, is it terribly red, or faint?
　　Do you use any blue? Is it Prussian?'

'I paint what I paint', said Rivera.

'Whose is that head that I see on my wall?'
　　Said John D.'s grandson Nelson.
　　'Is it anyone's head whom we know, at all?
　　A Rensselaer, or a Saltonstall?
　　Is it Franklin D. Is it Mordaunt Hall?
　　Or is it the head of a Russian?'

'I paint what I think', said Rivera.

78. Terry Schoonhaven. *Morning Room Mural*. 1985. 4·44 × 11·4 m (168 × 432 in). Federal Court of Appeals, Pasadena, California

'I paint what I paint, I paint what I see,
        I paint what I think,' said Rivera.
        'And the thing that is dearest in life to me
        In a bourgeois hall is Integrity;
        However . . . . . .
        I'll take out a couple of people drinkin'
        And put in a picture of Abraham Lincoln.
        I could even give you McCormick's reaper
        And still not make my art much cheaper.
        But the head of Lenin has got to stay
        Or my friends will give me the bird today,
        The Bird, the bird, forever'.

'It's not good taste in a man like me',
        Said John D.'s grandson Nelson
        'To question an artist's integrity
        Or mention a practical thing like a fee
        But I know what I like to a large degree,
        Though art I hate to hamper;
        For twenty-one thousand conservative bucks
        You paint a radical. I say shucks,
        I never could rent the offices—
        The capitalistic offices.
        For this, as you know, is a public hall
        And people want doves, or a tree in fall,
        And though your art I dislike to hamper,
        I owe a little to God and Gramper,
        And after all,
        It's my wall'.

'We'll see if it is', said Rivera.

79. Terry Schoonhaven and Vic Henderson. *Isle of California*. 1972. Enamel mural, 13·3 × 20·6 m (42 × 65 ft). Village Recorder Building, West Los Angeles, California

80. Jennifer Bartlett. *Swimmers Atlanta: Flare*. 1979. Installation in nine parts: oil on canvas; baked enamel and silkscreen grid; enamel on steel plates, 412 × 396 cm (156 × 150 in). Richard B. Russell Federal Building and United States Courthouse, Atlanta, Georgia

81. Jennifer Bartlett. *The Garden*. 1981. Oil on canvas, 238 × 174 cm (90 × 66 in); enamel on canvas, 246 × 127 cm (93 × 48 in); oil on mirror, 246 × 127 cm (93 × 48 in). Mr and Mrs Charles Saatchi

PROGRESSIVE MURALS

Impulse is very important in my work. I have a non-analytical approach to it and I don't want to break that freshness. To me art is about reaching a mood, a feeling on the unconscious level.—Ricardo Cinalli, muralist.

This chapter is concerned with artists who push forward the frontiers of mural painting. Argentinian artist Ricardo Cinalli's remark could apply to a number of his peers who are continually searching for new forms and original ways of expressing themselves. Their art does not obviously draw its inspiration from traditional sources. Past centuries of art have clearly had their influence on each generation of artists but, as Cinalli points out, 'We have just touched the tip of mural painting. Just as under the jungles of South America, there is a wealth of minerals and jewels to be found, so there is a universe of ideas and excitement to be discovered in the future of murals.'

Modern approaches to the art of mural painting vary enormously. The subject matter can range from powerful figurative imagery—conjured up by the dynamic New York-based Italian painter, Sandro Chia—to the abstracts of David Novros with their deep colours in continual movement. The range of mediums employed is enormous and offers endless scope for experiment: the conventional oil on canvas and wooden panels or waterbased paints on plaster; the mysterious fresco-like quality of Ricardo Cinalli's tissue and pastel murals; the metallic creations of Pamela Margonelli; the shimmering enamel on glass of Jennifer Bartlett.

How do these muralists survive at a time when there is a limited market for innovative, and especially abstract, murals? Unless they are extremely well known and in constant demand, wallpainting constitutes only part of their artistic output. Most muralists make a living, and also enjoy, working in other mediums. They nearly

82. Sandro Chia. *The Palio*.
1985–86. Acrylic
on canvas, four
412 × 982 cm
(156 × 372 in) panels.
Palio Restaurant,
Equitable Building,
New York

always concentrate on smaller-scale studio work—portraiture, easel paintings, illustrations, drawings—or they teach as they wait for the next commission.

Mark Wickham, the English artist, has always made a living painting portraits, but has only painted two large-scale murals. It takes years, especially in England, to become known as a talented muralist, unless the artist is an unusually good self-publicist. Recommendation is usually by word of mouth, which is slow, or publicity, which is rare. Artists are quite insular in their chosen profession and one of the attractions for many of them of doing a mural is the challenge of relating their work to architecture.

Many of the muralists in this chapter are well-known artists in other fields, such as Sandro Chia and the American painter Jennifer Bartlett, both of whom have emerged as two of the most important artists of the last decade. Chia, who was hailed at the 1980 Venice Biennale as the best of a new Italian wave of figurative expressionists, has produced one of the most exciting new murals in America for the Palio Restaurant in New York (Plate 82).

The theme, both for the restaurant and for Chia's work, is the Palio, a spectacular bi-annual horse race in Siena, that recreates the military and political glories of the Sienese republic of 1260–1555. Four walls are covered with bold, richly textured images from the race. Monumental muscle-bound men, horses and centaurs stampede round the wall. Preparations for the race, which only lasts ninety seconds, are a blaze of colours with the scarves, cords and banners flourished during the procession. The mural celebrates the event in all its medieval pageantry: the opening parade of horses and riders in traditional costume; the race; the laurels to the winners and the ritual baccanalia which follow. Chia represents the archetypal characters of the Sienese festival with figures from classical, Renaissance and modern art. His highly charged colours and bravura brushwork perfectly express the sense of revelry inherent in the Palio.

The versatility and broad scope of Bartlett's style, her subject matter, and the wide range of mediums she works in, are invigorating and innovative. The dining room in the London home of British collectors Doris and Charles Saatchi looks out through leaded windows into a small garden with a swimming pool. Inspired by a visit to Matisse's chapel in Vence while she was living in France in 1980, and longing to tackle an environment where she could include several paintings, Jennifer Bartlett covered the interior with nine distinct images of the garden, each in a different medium (Plate 81).

Every wall in the room is a reflection of the garden with the green of the leaves and the shimmering blue of the water. Using fresco and tile, oil on canvas, glass and mirror, enamel on enamelled steel plates, large-scale drawing and papier colle, each surface evokes the changing seasons. The soft greens of summer spill from the oil-on-glass image, and the undulating patterns of the water invite the onlooker down to swim in its blue-green depths. Next to it lies an autumnal image where fallen leaves lie upon the darkened water.

Elsewhere in London, in a seventeenth-century house once inhabited by Huguenot silk weavers in the district of Spitalfields, lives an artist of startling originality. Ricardo Cinalli was born in Argentina and he studied philosophy and psychology as well as music before launching himself into painting. Cinalli hoped he could combine the three disciplines in his paintings. He now says, 'In my work now you can see, of course, a great deal of my unconscious self but you cannot directly apply psychology to painting.' This is not an entirely convincing argument since his work is, at least partly, motivated by a strong fascination for all that is masculine, huge and heroic.

Cinalli creates monumental fresco-like drawings on tissue paper. The strength of the figures provides a striking contrast with the fragility of the technique. Inspired by the great luminosity of Tintoretto's paintings he wanted to explore the possibility of achieving vast areas of light using another medium. Visiting the Turkish baths,

83. Ricardo Cinalli. *Premonitions 1: Air*. 1985. Pastel on tissue paper, 375 × 220 cm
(142 × 83 in). Artist's collection

84. Ricardo Cinalli. *Premonitions 2: Fire*. 1986. Pastel on tissue paper, 370 × 220 cm
(140 × 83 in). Mr and Mrs Jay Bauer

85. Mark Wickham. 1985. Acrylic on hardboard, 31·68 × 1·74 m (100 ft × 5 ft 6 in). Le Champenois Restaurant, London

he was fascinated by figures walking by who would disappear into the mists after two metres, and realized that with pastels and several layers of tissue he could achieve the same effect.

Cinalli was also impressed with the scale of Egyptian sculpture, and started drawing and painting parts of the human body on a huge scale. His images are usually male. 'The female aspect of my art is the creation', he says, 'The strength of the drawings, and their volume, is in the muscles, the veins and the torsos which are better expressed by the male.' His paintings of the Four Elements are based on premonitions of disaster, a symbolic expression of a world gone mad. 'It is a way of camouflaging my own personal fears and inner turbulence,' says Cinalli, who strives to portray ugliness and fear through the intrinsic beauty in his painting. In the elemental painting *Air* a colossal pair of feet, symbol of the giant's invisible power, with veins as thick as ropes, appears to be floating, weightless, in the air. The giants are squeezing the life out of their hapless victims and a feeling of quiet terror reigns (Plate 83). This threatening power is also apparent in his second elemental painting *Fire* (Plate 84). Here the terrified horses are restrained by another gigantic superman, while the huddled masses in the background appear doomed.

Cinalli's technique for creating his race of giants is similar to that of a true fresco. The quickness of the pastel strokes has the same immediacy. He gradually builds up the five layers of transparent paper into a luminous image which continues to be both monumental and delicate. Each layer of numerous small pieces of paper must

86. Mark Wickham. 1985. Acrylic on hardboard, 31·68 × 1·74 m (100 ft × 5 ft 6 in). Le Champenois Restaurant, London

be completed before the whole five layers are pasted together. The transparency enables the underlying colour of the short curved strokes to be seen showing through successive layers. The immediacy of his paintings recalls the virtuosity of the old masters of fresco. 'The models for all my life drawings are all my friends,' says Cinalli with a mischievous smile. He dispenses with the tedium of squaring up his murals on the wall. He owns three small paint brushes, preferring to use his hands and a cloth to achieve the volume and shape of his images.

Another artist who pushes against the boundaries of conventional mural painting is the American colourist Pamela Margonelli. Inspired by the time-weathered patina of painted walls in Italy and the light, colours and textures of that country as well as the Caribbean, she creates shimmering atmospheric wall treatments, full of random scratched-on doodlings. These are taken subconsciously from the sgraffito techniques on old Baroque houses in southern Italy. 'Reflective qualities are what interest me, and surfaces that change with movement and light.'

The walls of the artist's loft in New York are alive with incandescent colour. A layer of metallic—gold or silver—or iridescent paint is first painted over plastered walls. Then, changing the tone to be lighter by the window, various overlays of tempera in the cooler colours of blue and green, rose or grey, are added, some of which is then wiped off. The metallic colour pushes through the flat paint, producing subtly observed highlights and reflections in the surfaces. Margonelli uses cool mossy green colours to balance the heat and energy of New York on the walls of her studio and paints the bottom of the walls to communicate the heat of Brazil or the haziness of a summer afternoon in Naples.

Progressive murals are mostly commissioned by private and publicly funded organizations, restaurants, hospitals and art institutions. Unless the client is an avid collector or a patron of the arts, such as the Saatchis, progressive murals by well-known artists are seldom found in people's houses. The often complex themes and vivid colouring tend to be too strong to live with.

Although murals in restaurants suffer from a high mortality rate, and often the loss is not great, occasionally one comes across a work so good that it should be preserved by law. One such mural was commissioned for Le Champenois, a French restaurant in the City of London, with a theme of French still life (Plates 85, 86). The wallpainting was executed by the well-known portrait painter Mark Wickham, who used to teach at Marlborough College with friend and fellow muralist, Richard Shirley Smith. Wickham comes from a long tradition of artists. Both his parents are painters who trained at the Royal Academy and his grandmother, Mabel Lucie Attwell, was the famous illustrator of children's books.

In the mural the artist works his way through a continual, slightly decadent gastronomic day, beginning with coffee and croissants and ending with post-prandial brandy in the bar of the restaurant. The composition is deceptively simple. As the angle of the painted table is so shallow, all the objects chosen had to present their best aspect as silhouettes. The mural has a crisp airy style and its thirty elaborately detailed, 4-foot by 5-foot panels are covered in predominantly pastel-coloured objects. Some of these have appeared before in Wickham's oil paintings: a French enamel coffee pot and a yoghurt carton favoured by Georgio Morandi, a painter much admired by Wickham. The coffee pot suggests a breakfast scene and takes up one third of the wall. The other two-thirds are divided between a mouth-watering cooking scene and a picnic late on a lazy summer afternoon—with people beginning to think about dinner. An orange has just been eaten and half a glass of champagne casually rests on the table. All the essential cooking ingredients and objects are at hand: eggs for making mayonnaise, a Greek tin oil jug and large cloves of garlic, bay leaves, a French sauceboat which balances the blue and white mixing bowl on the other side. The champagne has the restaurant owner's name on it and the nougat that of his partner.

Wickham wanted the atmosphere of the mural to be cool and to marry in with the brisk, clean architecture of the restaurant, designed by his brother. The two had long been looking for an opportunity to work together and the mural is one of the few examples in England where the architect and the muralist have collaborated on the design of the room from the outset of building. But why did he paint the objects so large? Everything is four times its natural size. 'I realized that I would be there for ten years unless I enlarged the still-life objects,' he replies.

Abstract murals are rarely sought by architects and their clients who mainly prefer more conventional figurative and architectural representation, historical and allegorical fantasies or romantic decoration. This aversion to the abstract with its bold use of pure colour is difficult to explain but it seems to be caused by three things. First, abstract art has never suited the Englishman's sensibilities, as opposed to those of the American. This idiosyncracy, combined with England's deep bond to historicism, conspires against the abstract artist. Second, many interiors are not suited to large splashes of colour. Lastly, it is due to a certain lack of courage and fear of the unknown among people who commission murals. There is also the fact that many artists who are drawn to the world of mural illusion are not abstract painters.

Modern American buildings, on the other hand, with the clean lines of their imaginative architecture, their large spaces and clearer light, are more suited to abstract art. Even buildings erected in the 1920s and 1930s

87. David Novros. 1983–84. Buon fresco. Federal Courthouse, Miami, Florida

88 Willie Fielding, Acrylic and fluorescent paint, 158 × 253 cm (60 × 96 in), Mrs Naz Alam

39. Leonard Rosoman, 1985–86. Acrylic. Royal Academy of Art, London.

90. (*previous page*) Pamela Margonelli. 1986. Tempera and metallic paint. Mel Furukawa

91. Kent Twitchell. *Emerson Woelffer*. 1980. Pencil on Hypro paper, 380 × 95 cm (144 × 36 in). Emerson Woelffer

92. Robert Hutchinson. 1986. Plaster, mud and natural pigment, 380 × 317 cm (144 × 120 in). Artist's collection

benefit from the unrestrained freedom of abstract art such as the work of David Novros, a New York artist who scorns the recent connection between 'artists' and 'architects'. He feels this has produced the 'visual equivalent of muzak in elevators'.

Novros, who communicates through vibrant non-imagistic painting, has transformed a 1930s Mediterranean-revival style federal courthouse in Miami, Florida, into a pulsating space of contrasting warm and cool colours (Plate 87). The project for the busiest courthouse in America with its huge volume of drug-related business involved painting more than 6300 square feet of walls, archways and ceilings of the loggias encircling the interior courtyard. Funded by the federal government's art-in-architecture programme, which allocates 1 per cent of a subsidized building's budget for art, the graceful limestone archway of the interior courtyard frames the mural. One of the few contemporary muralists to use the ancient and laborious technique of *fresco buono*, Novros needed all the wall surfaces replastered before he could begin painting. Drawing from a traditional palette the artist arranged all the colours of the wallpainting in a cyclical pattern, with brilliant tones of reds and blues gently changing to more sombre hues of greens and ochres.

Novros calls himself an itinerant artist and feels his ideas are best expressed in conditions that allow time and light to act directly with the painting. An avid crusader for mural rights, he states that 'Murals are not considered art because they are not connected with galleries and therefore cannot be resold.'

Prejudice against abstract murals also extends to fluorescent painting with its images of the 1960s. Willie Fielding, a product of that period known for his erotic paintings, is an English artist who admits to being well out of the main stream of any art movement. Striving to achieve a realistic three-dimensional effect with fluorescent paint is a difficult process. Colours change continually as day runs into night and they often have to be painted over four times, first in acrylics, then in fluorescent paint in complete darkness, with only a small black light to see by.

Fielding painted an infinitely detailed and mysterious rendition of the Persian poet Attar's *Conference of the Birds* for his client Naz Allam who fled Iran during the revolution in 1978 (Plate 88). It is the story of the hoopoe who said to all the other birds, 'You are wasting your time in pursuit of this life of idle pleasure and financial gain. You must come with me to find the *Simurgh*, the great god bird.' All the birds found an excuse not to follow the hoopoe. The hawk said he could not leave the arm of the prince, the nightingale refused to desert the rose and the cockatoo maintained his loyalty to the crown. Eventually, however, the hoopoe persuaded his friends to follow him on an epic journey through seven valleys, only three of which are shown in the painting.

The first valley, the valley of quest, is guarded by the dragon peacock, filling the birds with fear. This is followed by the valley of love, symbolized by moths around the flame. The third valley is the valley of regeneration, represented by the phoenix rising from the ashes. Only thirty birds have survived the journey when they finally arrive at their destination. The hoopoe declared, 'Here is the *Simurgh*', which, in Persian means thirty birds.

The human figure has always played an important part in the paintings and murals of Leonard Rosoman, whose prolific career stretches back to the 1930s. A fluent draughtsman and an energetic artist, he is at his best when painting subjects that deal with feelings. Many of his paintings are based on childhood incidents and personal memories recorded in diaries covering his years of travelling. He recalled one summer afternoon, as a young boy, hiding in some bushes near an orchard surrounded by sunflowers. In ran a man and a woman shouting, who promptly started to hit each other. Fifteen years later, Rosoman, who had enjoyed the secrecy of being alone and seeing the drama while appearing invisible, spontaneously painted the angry man and the woman naked. Although she was clothed at the time, she seemed naked to him in her vulnerability. 'My paintings are essentially situational, both emotionally and pictorially,' says Rosoman.

93. Edward Schmidt. *Towards Bethesda Fountain*. 1985. Acrylic on canvas, 222 × 444 cm (84 × 168 in). Alwyn Court, New York

Modern dress in murals looks dowdy, unless amusingly stylized as in a striking new mural painted by Rosoman. It is based on an *Upstairs Downstairs* view of life in London's Royal Academy of Art (Plate 89). He depicts *Upstairs* as a private view of the Summer Exhibition, with excited art lovers meeting in the foyer and converging on the paintings. The unseen world of the Royal Academy Schools lies in the two architectural lunettes *Downstairs*, with the students seen busily working in a life class. The second lunette shows the Schools corridor lined with slightly menacing antique casts which threatened Rosoman when he was a student.

Kent Twitchell, a Los Angeles photorealist, uses an old billboard technique of pouncing large-scale drawings onto the wall and then chalking in the holes. Interest in this work soared after he had completed a huge outdoor mural of Steve McQueen's face in 1971. He now concentrates on painting gigantic people on the interior walls of their houses.

Twitchell has a passion about the stone sarcophagus and he devised a method of portraying giant 12-foot portraits of people which are pulled out of a box on the floor (Plate 91). He says he wanted the sense of the drawings growing out of the ground 'like a tree to give them more power'. For this reason none of these thick, dramatic drawings of people have feet—'almost like architecture pulled out of the earth,' he says. The pores and veins stand out in the minutely detailed hands and Twitchell likes the notion of his strange giants, with their similarities to the mysterious stone sculptures of Easter Island and Stonehenge, standing around Los Angeles looking down at the community.

A composition of interrelating figures is also the theme of a striking new mural full of colour and strong flowing lines by a talented although relative newcomer to the world of murals, Edmund Caswell. Under the bequest of Sir James Barrie, creator of *Peter Pan*, Great Ormond Street Hospital for Sick Children owns the copyright to the stories of the little boy who never grew up. Funds from these royalties helped finance a 72-foot long mural full of loosely drawn figures. 'I decided from the outset not to include childish drawings just because it was a children's hospital, but to draw the characters as lifelike as possible', explained Caswell. In a memory-provoking mural, full of vigorous movement and swashbuckling action, the outward and return journeys of Peter Pan and the Darling children appear in dreamlike sequences (Plate 99).

The world of progressive murals is often closely linked to contemporary architecture and interior design. The very nature of contemporary architecture can appear cold and hostile without the addition of art. Robert Hutchinson, the inventive San Francisco interior designer, has always wanted to live in a mud house. He creates sculpturesque, flowing spaces and works physically and enthusiastically with his 'family'—the plasterer, the carpenter and the stonemason. His apartment is painted in warm, earth colours with the rounded contours of a simple adobe dwelling made out of natural materials, including mud. 'Design is the easiest thing in the world—although I refuse to compromise on it—it's the execution that's hard,' says Hutchinson. His huge collection of ancient and primitive objects and artifacts from many parts of the world stands prominently against a background of decorative friezes of plaster and driftwood bas-reliefs and sculptured wallpaintings of mud coloured with natural earth dyes (Plate 92).

American artist Edward Schmidt's mural *Toward Bethesda Fountain* is a tribute to his friend, the artist Milet Andrejevic, who painted the original (Plate 93). The reworked composition is painted in muted tones of green, blue and grey and evokes a rustic woodland where a serene pace of life is enjoyed by three adolescent boys. Schmidt painted the mural with the assistance of students in the New York Academy of Art's Mural Atelier, of which he is the director.

94. Ricardo Cinalli. *Human Landscape*. 1986. Oil on board, 400 × 400 cm (152 × 152 in). Henley Festival

95. (*overleaf*) Robert Jackson. 1972. Watercolour, 950 × 950 × 475 cm (360 × 360 × 180 in). Mrs Ann Getty, San Francisco, California

96. (*overleaf*) Robert Jackson. 1980. Acrylic, 475 × 475 × 222 cm (180 × 180 × 84 in). Artist's collection

ROMANTIC AND DECORATIVE MURALS

We may not want to admit it and it may be hidden under layers of subterfuge, but most of us have a romantic streak. Romantic illusion is what most people want when they commission a mural for their home. It allows them to escape from reality into a world of fantasy, mystery and even frivolity. In an opening scene of a play or ballet, the audience may be enthralled by the curtains rising on a fairytale theatrical setting. In the same way, a backcloth of romantic escapism in the home also serves to soothe stressful lives and evoke a visual sense of pleasure. As Henri Matisse said, 'Art should be something like a good armchair in which to rest from physical fatigue.'

The essence of romanticism remains constant but its definition changes with the evolution of art, architecture and decoration. The very first attempts at interior design were the murals which embellished homes in classical times. Today nearly half a century of unromantic modernism has rekindled a nostalgia for sumptuous and picturesque imitations in much the same way as an eighteenth-century grandee might have built a Gothick folly to escape the rigidity of Palladianism. Commissioning murals though, is no longer just a pastime for the very rich, who have always enjoyed scenic landscapes, capricci (whimsical and fanciful works of art) and cartouches in their homes. Although architects are becoming more involved, most murals in residences are commissioned by interior designers.

The current passion for overdecorating with numerous different paint effects has not seen such popularity since the mid-nineteenth century. The problem with the word 'decorative' is that it has acquired a superficiality which is not always justified. The fashion for ragging and dragging, stipling and marblizing everything in sight—often at iniquitous cost—tends to be associated with frilly bedrooms and rouched blinds. This tendency has rubbed off on purely decorative murals, some of which (the 'geranium and trellis school') are frankly bad, because neither the client nor the muralist understands the complexities of good wallpainting. On the other hand the skill and imagination of many muralists whose work is primarily decorative takes them far beyond the realms of interior decoration. It would be sad if people turned against decorative murals as a reaction to the mediocrity which will, inevitably, creep into the medium as demand for murals grows.

97. Robert Walker. 1971. Acrylic, 2·85 × 14·26 m (9 × 45 ft). Richard Booth

98. Robert Walker. 1971. Acrylic, 2·85 × 14·26 m (9 × 45 ft). Richard Booth

A preoccupation with flowers, foliage and the popular 'sky ceilings', which date back to classical times, has always been a feature of decorative murals and trompe l'oeil. The simple flower is a powerful and enduring symbol of both romance and beauty. The spreading interest in natural history in the mid-fifteenth century produced exquisite books which were finely illustrated with miniature flowers, birds, animals, butterflies and other insects, for rich patrons with a love of nature and art. One of the finest examples of decorative borders with this detailed observation of plant life, is a Book of Hours commissioned around 1477 by a wealthy patron, Engelbert of Nassau, for his private devotions; it now rests in the Bodleian Library, Oxford. The artist's name is unknown but it is believed to be the work of the Master of Mary of Burgundy.

This quiet devotion to nature shines through in the quintessentially romantic murals of Robert Jackson, one of America's best-known decorative artists. Jackson has been painting murals for the past thirty years—eight of them in England in the 1950s working for Oliver Messel and John Siddeley. Jackson is versatile and approaches his work armed with a deep knowledge of the given style or period. He is particularly fond of the dark landscapes and still lifes of the seventeenth-century French and Italian paintings. The mural in the dining room of his country house in upstate New York, is based on the primitive styles of the itinerant landscape painters in early nineteenth-century America (Plate 96). Jackson captures the simplicity of this type of folk art, the work of housepainters and journeyman stencillers in New England homes, with the bold use of blues and greens which blend harmoniously over the walls. He conveys an impression of space between the seemingly endless river and sky with a landscape sparsely dotted with simple indigenous trees. Jackson is a friendly and hospitable man who enjoys entertaining friends at the weekends. He says, 'A dining room can be far more festive than other rooms in the house, simply because you don't live in it.'

Jackson's work is mostly commissioned by interior decorators, who admire his talent for meticulously detailed decorations as well as his recreations of clouds and *faux marbre*. He surmises that murals in England are less often commissioned through decorators because the English have, traditionally, been more discriminating, and feel confident in their own judgements on art for their homes. Jackson's attention to detail and his infinite patience elevate a mural done for Mrs Ann Getty in the dining room of her San Francisco home with its panoramic view of the bay, from the purely decorative to something approaching fine art (Plate 95). Inspired by the antique Chinese wallpapers in London's Victoria and Albert Museum, Jackson has recreated them perfectly to complement the room's chinoiserie design. Painted in watercolour to emulate the originals as far as possible, the room is covered in delicately coloured flowers, trees and birds.

Our fascination with plants, combined with a desire to enlarge our urban living spaces, has resulted in the addition of real or imaginary conservatories. The glass variety, with its feeling of luxurious simplicity, is ideal for use as a dining room. According to the writer Shirley Hibberd (1823–90), the Victorian conservatory, apart from being a glass-covered garden, was seen as 'a place for frequent resort and agreeable assemblage at all seasons and especially at times of festivity'. Decorative murals can make these even prettier, an effect achieved by Tony Raymond at Ranelagh Cottage in the heart of London's Chelsea (Plate 100). Bright splashes of greenery envelop the room, interspersed with the buildings which originally surrounded the cottage. The eighteenth-century European upper classes were fond of keeping dressed-up monkeys, and the soft colours of the conservatory are brightened by the sartorial creature playing with a mask.

The imagined conservatory, on the other hand, can only be achieved through the skilful use of trompe l'oeil, Ian Cairnie's speciality. Cairnie has successfully achieved this in a small room in London where, with perfect perspective, he leads the eye back through the doors into the middle distance. A make-believe con-servatory, full of greenery and a table, precisely planted, conveys a sense of order and neatness, a peaceful place

99. Edmund Caswell. *The Journey of Peter Pan*. 1981–87. Acrylic, 2·53 × 22·8 m (8 × 72 ft). Hospital for Sick Children, Great Ormond Street, London (unfinished)

100. Tony Raymond. 1987. Flashe, 2·53 × 10·77 m (8 × 34 ft). Mr Giles Swarbreck

101. Ian Cairnie. 1983. Acrylic, 301 × 444 cm (114 × 168 in). Nicole Karen

102. Robin Archer. 1983. Acrylic. Private collection

103. Priscilla Kennedy. 1985. Acrylic, 380 × 380 cm (144 × 144 in). Mrs Cherry Hambro

104. Priscilla Kennedy. 1985. Acrylic, 380 × 380 cm (144 × 144 in). Mrs Cherry Hambro

for study and meditation and perhaps the modern equivalent of the scholar's cell so often portrayed in the fifteenth century (Plate 101).

The illusion of living in another country is another popular escape. Morocco seems to be a great favourite for those who want an exotic mural in their house. A sheikh from the Arab Emirates wanted a mural from the English artist Robin Archer which would blend in with the rest of the Arab decor in his London flat; Archer included some of the client's numerous other residences in the Middle East (Plate 102). The small hallway leading off the main dining room has been transformed into a turquoise Moroccan anteroom. Archer, a theatre designer for twenty years, comments, 'You pick up every conceivable trick from stage designing and learn to be a good magpie. I cut stencils for all the Moroccan designs and the "Moucharabiyeh" screening. I didn't paint any of the background in first at all, but instead just lined the horizon up.' The design for the screening was first stencilled in in very dark blue acrylic. When tackling the background seen through the screening, the artist painted over the design, so the stencil would keep coming through as a shadow. In a long, time-consuming process, this enabled him to keep the fretwork without spoiling the finished painting of the background.

Floral compositions in murals and trompe l'oeil are often dismissed as just 'pretty paintings', and sometimes rightly. But there are many examples of bold plants and foliage making a striking impact in a room. The dramatic use of colour, so often used by the West Coast painters in their murals, enhances the effect. Los Angeles-based artist Robert Walker has achieved this with considerable success for his client Richard Booth of San Francisco (Plates 97, 98). An artist who enjoys painting natural and over-scaled plant forms, Walker depicts massive fronds and a profusion of tropical plants which literally engulf the narrow bedroom. Against this dramatic backdrop, here and there a butterfly hovers, a ladybird crawls slowly up an endless road of green and out of the dense greenery slithers an unsuspecting snake.

For obvious reasons 'nature' murals appeal to city dwellers for whom the illusion of the countryside is a necessary antidote to their urban lives. A fine example of this necessary unreality can be seen in the house and garden of the eccentric and bohemian artist Roy Alderson, who has spent much of his energies in the last four decades tirelessly exploring the trickeries of trompe l'oeil. The result fills every corner of his Chelsea home in London. Alderson has an inherent sense of drama. The house is a combination of pure theatre, an ingenious understanding of technology and imaginative craftsmanship.

Behind the terracotta and blue Rococo fantasy featuring a lady sphinx with her parasol, inspired by bits and pieces taken from various Bavarian castles and palaces, lie cupboards stacked with paints and paintbrushes, tools, materials and books (Plate 105). This is the hub of Alderson's studio by day. At night the room is transformed into a romantic dining room presided over by a lady with the lamp and complete with a seascape blind which fills the window's arched surround, a trompe l'oeil painted in grisaille. Alderson always tones down the richness of the colours by adding a good deal of white to his paint.

Many of the original murals in this magical house, including the dining room table top, were painted on marblized melamine. The finished mural was then returned to the melamine factory where they put macaroon paper on top, rather like tissue impregnated with resin; after this the entire mural was flattened out by huge presses, giving it a totally smooth appearance.

Alderson is an original. In 1936 he opened an antique shop on London's King's Road in Chelsea and once owned a London cab handpainted in pink, button-studded trompe l'oeil. The two greatest influences on Alderson's work were Rex Whistler's decorations at the Tate Gallery in London and the Papiers Peints of the early nineteenth century with their imagery of lush trees, natives and romantic scenery. His exotic bedroom is like a blast of tropical sunshine. Painted in oil, enormous palm leaves spread over the walls and ceilings, handles

105. Roy Alderson. 1964. Oil, 253 × 507 cm (96 × 192 in). Artist's collection

metamorphose into parrots, and a secret portion of the flowered wall hides the television. The eighteenth-century mirror with its classically painted top panel is flanked by lamps to which real scallop shells are attached as shades. The realistic inlaid ivory on the small chest beside the mirror is, in fact, penwork done by the artist (Plate 106).

Murals combined with decorative finishes and special tricks such as distressing and antiquing are much in vogue at the moment. When subtly united in the right context, it can heighten the purpose and feeling of the romantic mural. 'Antiquing' is the process of imitating the paint patina acquired over many years. The term 'distressing' means to age a wall or piece of furniture by sanding off layers of paint to show the plaster or wood underneath, resulting in a wall whose appearance is not uniform.

In a small room in Sandra Cooke's bewitching house in London, Bruce Church, a native of New York, has created a little piece of Morocco, a favourite haunt of its owner (Plate 107). As the artist points out, 'Learning about the architecture and culture of unknown countries through books when designing a mural is an enjoyable side benefit of mural painting. After a few weeks of delving into the painted subject, it becomes easier to pick out the small details and relevant motifs connected with the particular country.' The main wall of Church's mural is of a peaceful scene of nomadic Bedouin with their camels. The terracotta earth colours of the walls were distressed, partly with a paint brush and partly with rags, which the artist tends to use frequently. Different Moroccan tiles are

106. Roy Alderson. 1964. Oil, 253 × 507 cm (96 × 192 in). Artist's collection

placed round the bottom third of the wall, simulating the mismatching of tiles common to that country. Above the painted grill windows the opening passage from the Koran 'There is but one God and his name is Allah' rounds off the romantic illusion.

Stonemasonry in the form of niches, pillars and balustrades is the stock-in-trade of contemporary muralists. The use of balustrades as an architectural motif can be found in murals dating back to the fourteenth century. One simple example which included naked house knights and elegantly dressed ladies leaning over the balustrade, was painted in the latter part of the century in the castle of Roncolo at Bolzano, high in the Tyrolean Alps. Since trompe l'oeil was significantly cheaper and could achieve similar effects as real architecture, it was popular with a highly artistic and sophisticated society who needed an extra element of fantasy in their villas. In a London dining room, Jonathan Brunskill has captured a sense of intimacy and enclosure, using the ubiquitous balustrade (Plate 108). The miniature orange trees on either side of the empty birdcage resting on its deep burgundy velvet drape conveys an atmosphere of orderliness. This is heightened by the straight lines of the balustrade together with the obelisk, privet hedge and Greek temple quietly standing in the well-manicured garden.

Past glories in the form of historical battle scenes or romantic ancestral legends are best suited to large

107. Bruce Church. Oil, 253 × 317 cm (96 × 120 in). Sandra Cooke

108. Jonathan Brunskill. 1985–86. Oil, 253 × 317 cm (96 × 120 in). Private collection

and ancient family homes. In the past two centuries aristocrats and the wealthy upper classes, especially the Irish, with their strong romantic streak, built mock castles, complete with turrets and battlements, as a form of romantic illusion on a grand scale. Commissioning castles is no longer in vogue and the cheaper solution is to own a mural which evokes the heroic heritage.

In the Great Hall of Layer Marnay, an historical building in Essex, Priscilla Kennedy's mural *Battle of the Spurs* tells the story of Lord Marnay (Plate 116). A companion-at-arms of Henry VIII, he planned to build a great house, but only managed the stables and an eight-storey gatehouse before dying in 1523. The 22-foot by 10-foot mural, which is painted in oils, rests in the entrance hall of the thatched barn, part of the original stables. In the foreground Lord Marnay, who led the rearward in the battle in northern France, is accompanied by his standard bearer. After a first unsuccessful siege against the French, Henry VIII, who led the midward, and Cardinal Wolsey, with his yellow and blue banner in front, were joined by the Emperor Maximilian. He can be seen to the left of the mural in yellow battle dress. Under the onslaught, the French dropped their supplies and food—in the front—and are seen fleeing over the hills.

Priscilla Kennedy is one of a handful of good successful women decorative mural painters in England. Trained in Florence for three years where she was taught tonal drawing by the famous Signora Simi, she can turn her hand to almost any type of mural painting. Most of her work is done in large country houses in Shropshire where she lives. Michelangelo's opinion that wallpainting was the 'manly art' would appear to apply to the scarcity

144

109. Felix Kelly. *Kelly's Passage, Fairlawn*. 1955. Oil on canvas, 444 × 634 cm (168 × 240 in).
       Private collection

110. Graham Rust. 1985. Flashe, 539 × 253 cm (204 × 96 in). Private collection

111. Graham Rust. 1985. Flashe, 539 × 253 cm (204 × 96 in). Private collection

112. Robert Jackson. 1986. Acrylic, 285 × 475 cm (108 × 180 in). Private collection

114. Roy Alderson. 1978. Oil, 253 × 127 cm (96 × 48 in).
Mrs J.E. Kelley, OBE

113. Richard Neas. 1975. Acrylic, 634 × 634 cm
(240 × 240 in). Private collection

116. Priscilla Kennedy. *Battle of the Spurs*. 1980. Acrylic, 317 × 697 cm (120 × 264 in). Mr Gerald Charrington

115. Felix Kelly. 1955. Oil on canvas. Private collection

117. Graham Rust. 1971. Flashe. Count Mirrlees

119. Priscilla Kennedy. 1981. Acrylic, 855 × 507 cm (324 × 192 in). Mr and Mrs David Scott

121. Richard Neas. 1980. Acrylic on glass, 285 × 158 cm
(108 × 60 in). Artist's collection

120. Jean Harvey. 1986. Oil, 475 × 317 cm
(180 × 120 in). Artist's collection

122. Lincoln Seligman. 1985. Acrylic, 285 × 158 cm
(108 × 60 in). Private collection

of contemporary women muralists. Painting murals is a demanding pastime. Long hours, physical endurance for painting large areas of wallspace and the constant running up and down of scaffolding takes its toll. This, plus the necessity of childbearing, has resulted in fewer well-known women muralists, compared to their male counterpart.

Graham Rust's theatrical mural painted for Count Mirrlees is another example where history and fiction blend easily (Plate 117). It is based on Patrick Leigh Fermor's story *The Violins of Saint Jacques*, about a French island resembling Haiti, where a glamorous and decadent life was shattered by a volcano erupting in the middle of Mardi Gras. Count Mirrlees is portrayed as a reclining Toussaint L'Ouverture, and his slaves bear the real names of those belonging to his ancestors. The latter had escaped the horrors of the French Revolution to find new identities and start plantations on San Domingo. Graham Rust has included not only his clients' family but also their friends, in a combination of figures, symbols, initials and jokes. Personalized murals should be fun—a combination of skill, wit and humour.

Owen Turville, who worked for many years with John Fowler, England's most acclaimed decorator of the century, takes a more conventional, but no less effective, approach. His use of colour and numerous decorative techniques are given free rein in the London home of Lord Carrington, a former British Foreign Secretary and Secretary General of NATO (Plate 124). Turville has created an exact replica of the Carringtons' country home in Buckinghamshire. The garden, in the full glory of an English summer, is painted onto a 20-foot wall directly outside the dining-room windows. Against a background of barns and a small white gazebo surrounded by herbaceous borders and flowering bushes, two nineteenth-century Japanese bronze herons wade in a pool just out of sight, while the Carringtons' two dogs gambol across the manicured grass.

A good example of uninhibited fun is the London home of the American artist Jean Harvey. Inspired by intricately detailed miniatures, her dining room has been transformed into an enchanted Persian garden (Plate 120). Carefree flowers, oriental trees bulging with ripened fruit, birds and a brook full of leaping fish stretch all round the room. The magical atmosphere tends to have a hypnotic effect on guests who revel in dining in such an exotic cocoon. The mural brings into focus just how many of us are amateur decorators at heart. These spontaneous endeavours often result in some of the most appealing decorations of the 1980s.

123. Priscilla Kennedy. 1981. Acrylic, 2·69 × 10·13 m (8 ft 6 in × 32 ft). Mr John Reed

124. Owen Turville (in collaboration with John Fowler and Jean and Mark Hornak). Acrylic on cement and fibreglass, 317 × 634 cm (120 × 240 in). Lord Carrington

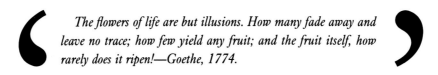

The flowers of life are but illusions. How many fade away and leave no trace; how few yield any fruit; and the fruit itself, how rarely does it ripen!—Goethe, 1774.

England and America abound in exciting, original and skilful contemporary murals. I have tried to include the best in this book, although there are bound to be some unheralded masters working quietly away whom I have overlooked. The oversight was unintentional and I hope they will forgive me. Of those I discovered, so many were of a high order that the final choice was very difficult. In the end this was dictated by the need to balance romantic illusion and innovation.

What does the future hold for the mural? To a large extent this will depend on the interaction between the architect, the muralist and the interest or indifference shown by the public. What follows is not meant to be a prescription for the future, but a few observations which may help to focus attention on some of the areas of neglect.

Art can only progress if it has an intellectual and spiritual driving force behind it. Muralists should be encouraged, starting at art school, to search for new forms of expression. As Alan Potter, head of the Mural Department at London's Chelsea School of Art, says, 'For the future of murals, I would like to see academics stop insisting that students be painters or sculptors. They should just get back into being artists. But I fear that mine is a Utopian view and it's a long time away.'

There are some interesting differences between the way in which the art is developing in the United States and Britain. The standards of purely decorative work are extremely high in America, where the wealthy are prepared to pay for the very best, but the British take more time and care in executing a mural. Some American muralists tend to have less staying power and want to complete their work quickly, before losing interest. On the other hand, while the technique and quality of most British muralists may be superior, the flair and lack of inhibition of the Americans, especially those on the West Coast, produce a large amount of exciting work. Ultimately what is needed is the vision of the Old Masters combined with the restless energy of modern art to record the age we live in with candour and imagination. Nostalgia is important but, with the pace of life changing so rapidly, muralists should be encouraged to explore the outer limits of their craft.

Governments, too, could do more. Muralists in America have been more fortunate than their English counterparts in this respect. The WPA programme helped artists in the 1930s. Public funding of the visual arts, for example, the Art-in-Architecture programme, provides for the embellishment of buildings all over the country. England could usefully follow America's example by making murals for corporations tax exempt. Apart from encouraging employment in the arts, it would greatly improve dour office interiors.

Established art circles in England could try not to look down their nose at murals. Major artists, as well as decorative artists, would appreciate the opportunity to work on public buildings. Many muralists have an uphill struggle getting the art world to take their work seriously, not always for sound, aesthetic reasons.

Local councils could do more to give the artist and the community a shared sense of purpose. Contemporary public murals are too often stuck on a wall without relating to their environment. Architects could call in muralists at the planning stages of a building more frequently, so that the design of the room leads up to, and focuses on, the mural. The best mural painting has to have a subject matter beyond itself, beyond its form, relating to a shared set of standards and beliefs. In classical times, the architect, the painter and the sculptor shared a common philosophy and this shared outlook was apparent in the consistency of their masterpieces. Today's artists could do worse than to follow their example.

158

SELECT BIBLIOGRAPHY

HANS FEIBUSCH, *Mural Painting*, Adam and Charles Black, 1946.

MARTIN BATTERSBY, *Trompe L'Oeil*, Academy Editions, 1974.

KURT WEHLTE, *The Materials and Technique of Painting*, Van Nostrand Reinhold, 1975.

M.L. D'ORANGE MASTAI, *Illusion in Art*, Abaris Books, 1975.

E.H. GOMBRICH, *Means and Ends: Reflections on the History of Fresco Painting*, Thames & Hudson, 1976.

E.H. GOMBRICH, *The Story of Art*, Phaidon, 1978.

CELESTINE DARS, *Images of Deception*, Phaidon, 1979.

RICHARD HAAS, *An Architecture of Illusion*, Rizzoli, 1981.

MIRIAM MILMAN, *Trompe L'Oeil Painting*, Skira, 1982.

CHARLES MCCORQUODALE, *The History of Interior Decoration*, Phaidon, 1983.

EDWARD LUCIE-SMITH, *Art of the 1930s*, Weidenfeld and Nicolson, 1985.

MIRIAM MILMAN, *Trompe-L'Oeil-Painted Architecture*, Rizzoli, 1986.

MICHAEL LEVEY, *Giambattista Tiepolo*, Yale University Press, 1986.

INDEX

INDEX

The author and publishers would like to thank all the Muralists, for the reproduction of their works, and also the museums and private owners who have kindly allowed works in their collections to be photographed. Acknowledgement for specific photographs is made to the following: Plate 5, Scala; 9, Michael Holford; 21, 29, John Gates; 28, Richard Bryant; 30, 33, John R. Simmons; 35, Peter Mauss; 44, James Mortimer; 62, Stan Ries; 69, Peter Moss; 71, Wyatt McSpadden; 91 Tessa Traeger; 93, Stanley Garth; 102, Fritz von der Schulenberg; 104, P. J. Gates Ltd; 115, Martin Fine/Forer.

"I Paint What I See" is from *Poems & Sketches of E. B. White*. © 1933 by E. B. White. Reprinted by permission of Harper & Row, Publishers, Inc.

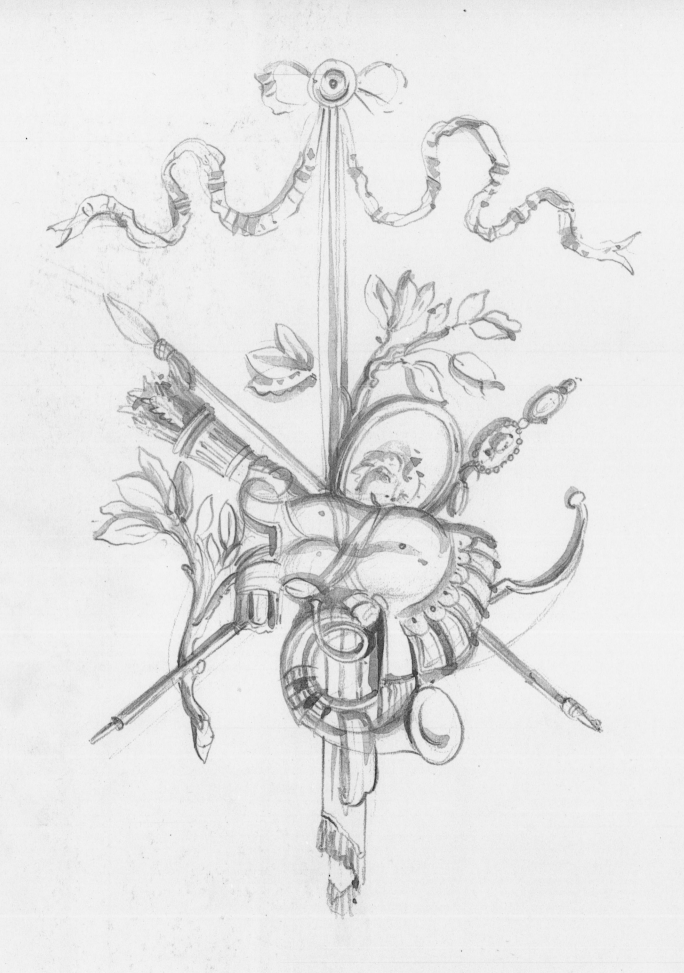